Unexplained Mysteries

Amazing Unsolved World Phenomenon

(Mind-boggling and Unsolved Mysteries through History)

Steve Solberg

Published By **Simon Dough**

Steve Solberg

Unexplained Mysteries: Amazing Unsolved World Phenomenon (Mind-boggling and Unsolved Mysteries through History)

ISBN 978-0-9949175-9-1

Legal & Disclaimer

The information contained in this book is not designed to replace or take the place of any form of medicine or professional medical advice. The information in this book has been provided for educational & entertainment purposes only.

The information contained in this book has been compiled from sources deemed reliable, and it is accurate to the best of the Author's knowledge; however, the Author cannot guarantee its accuracy and validity and cannot be held liable for any errors or omissions. Changes are periodically made to this book. You must consult your doctor or get professional medical advice before using any of the suggested remedies, techniques, or information in this book.

Table Of Contents

Chapter 1: What Happened Really?

On Christmas Eve, 2002 Lacey Peterson who was eight months pregnant with her first baby was reported missing from her home town in Modesto, California on April 13th of 2003. The bodies of Lacy as well as the son she had with her Connor were discovered lying on the shores of Sanford. It's a quarter one mile from the other.

What did happen to Laci or Conner? What happened to a happy, normal mom and her incredibly awaited son have their lives destroyed at such a young age. It's not clear why. the husband of Lacy is Scott Peterson is currently sitting on the death row following being indicted for the murders of his baby child and wife.

He's not stopping at claiming his innocence. After 13 years of having been found guilty of murder He appealed the verdict and claimed his lawyers had a problem with his trial and asked for an appeal. I must say that the parallels in the events that took place in the case of Lacy Scott Peterson and Lacy Scott Peterson and what happened with Shannon and Chris Watts are sometimes almost terrifying as I read about the case.

Again. I did a little research on the Peterson case several years ago just a few years after the first time it happened. and I recollected a great deal of things from the case, however, I didn't remember the details. as I go through the little details. being aware of how deeply entangled I was with the Watts case, and knowing that I was pretty well aware regarding this case. But it was when the facts struck me in a settling email manner.

What a similarity these events and, in particular, how comparable the women's murders were. The relationship dynamics as well as their general lives, what the husbands did prior to and following the murders is as if I'm revisiting the Watts murder case over and over. That's right. Please bear with me. From time to time, I'll time to time I will make a post and then say that this makes me like Chris Watson.

We're not trying remove anything from Lacey Peterson at all, however, it's amazing the similarities between them. Naturally Chris Watts for me is a worse case due to the nature of Bella as well as Celeste, Chris is. Chris and his daughters also perished. It just seems like it's much tougher and require an even greater amount of psychopath.

A cold-hearted murderer has killed the two daughters have raised over the decades. But it's hard to imagine what it would take for an icy-hearted psychopath to take his wife's life and the child she's expecting with. You know what I'm talking about? Right. I'm sure you'll arrive, you who are inclined to sift through every word I've said"Oh, but Chris Watts is worse than Scott Peterson.

It seems like you're on the Scott Peterson side. That's obviously not my intention. It's my opinion that you'd need a much worse person to do like Chris Watts did. Now let's get on with it You guys are aware of how I go about it to gain a better understanding of who someone is, what drives them to do these things and their character, as well as their manner of speaking.

It is necessary to go back to the very beginning, the time they were children together with Scott Peterson. The feeling I got was that I needed to travel back further. In 1945, on the 20th of December the man identified as John H Latham was struck by pipe, and then killed at a cost of $200 by a former employee of his salvage yard owned by him located in San Diego, California.

He was a husband and father of four. His sole daughter Jackie was two years old and half years old when he was killed. After Jackie's death, her mother suffered mental health issues due to the trauma from losing her husband an unforgiving manner and then being left with four kids to care for. Then she took the four children and placed them at the Nazareth home, which was essentially an orphanage because Jackie was the sole girl who was not able to be with her three brothers.

Now imagine this toddler girl who's 2 1/2 years old. My Bella's age. She lost her father. And then her mother. Her three brothers, all of which sure it was like a few hours for her. That would be very traumatic. This is especially true at this time. It was Jackie at Peterson, Scott Peterson's mom. ten years later, at age 13 Jackie returned to her mother's home after which her mother Helen passed away shortly following Jackie was graduated.

On the 17th January in 1962 Jackie floated around this point, seeking affection and to give it to the men that didn't deserve the love. Soon after, she became pregnant with her baby boy, Don, and after the father of the child left her, she offered Donald to adoption in the month of April, 1963. Then she became pregnant again with a second baby this time with a girl named Anne in the year 1964.

The dad of Anne was involved in a relationship with a different woman, and didn't wish to share anything with Jackie or the daughter of Jackie. Therefore, Jackie offered Anna to adoption too. Then, in July of 1965 she gave birth to a new child, only to be left by the father of this baby and mother.

After she was told at the doctor's appointment that she was expecting, doctors stared at her and said"Hey, Lady I'm telling you this time is like when you should likely keep this pregnancy. It's not enough to keep giving. You have kids that are available to be adopted. Have you considered raising one of them? It seems like that my Siri impressions are working, even when I'm not and I'm also able to make the impression of an oven.

That's exactly the result when I attempt to request Siri what the correct pronunciation of LA Jolla, California, my Google home, and Siri begin arguing over which is the most superior. It's a bit bizarre. It was then that Jackie went from being a single mom to a married one and started a dress boutique located in LA Jolla, California called the podium. There was a rumor that she frequently brought her son John on her way for work. His requirements were often neglected in the interest of the company.

However, I'm not sure whether this is true. People have said it. She was a friend of Lee Peterson, worst father of three. Lee had a very low childhood and was employed by the trucking industry before beginning the successful packing and delivering company within San Diego, California. Lee was embarrassed by his modest beginnings, and put in efforts to disguise his humble beginnings. started from scratch.

The expense of acquiring fancy cars as well as expensive houses, which naturally resulted in financial stress. Lee was described as introverted by his family as a face. Therefore, the people who had the best knowledge of him were describing him as insecure an introvert, wasn't sure if I knew him as very well. He wasn't a great emotional person. There is speculation that his first marriage failed because it was difficult for him to be with his children.

As if he had an interest in interfacing with them. Jackie and Lee were married. They adopted their son, John And a few months after that, on October 24, 1973, Scott Peterson was brought to the world. He was born via C-section. He was put on oxygen and removed from his mother shortly when he was born due to his pneumonia was present.

Scott was to be referred to as"the golden boy" to the family as well as his siblings as well as his parents although Jackie had a son while Lee Peterson had three children, Scott was clearly their most loved and put in a position of honor. The mother of Scott fondly be reminded that he took some time to master the art of walking walk, as there was always someone walking around in the year 1976.

The time when Scott was in his family. We moved to the scripts ranch. It was a much nicer suburb within San Diego than they were now living in. LA Jolla. Lee was often taking little Scott along to take care of packages. He said that it felt that he'd got small friend with him. It made him feel like he wasn't all alone.

The father also tried to make Scott engaged in activities that he enjoyed including hunting, fishing and golf in particular. He also explained that the reason he enrolled his son into these activities as well as bringing his son to work was that the reason he that it was more convenient for Scott to be able to enjoy spending time together with him as well as be able to connect with him.

If Scott was into his interests and hobbies, he would be interested in exactly the same activities that Lee loved to do. This is basically trying to make someone look like your own to make you prefer them since you enjoy you more. This is what I have gotten out of it. However, I might be wrong. Jackie is his son's older brother. was in trouble at high school. His family disowned him completely and removed him from the state and into family members.

Let's take a moment to unpack this briefly. It's not clear the sort of trouble John had to go through. There's a chance that it was really serious and his family scolded his involvement in the trouble during high school. It is quite common for students who are in high school to have trouble with. I was in trouble for a long time and sent him off to a different place.

Yet Scott was put on a high pedestal and brought together with his father, to work. He taught him how to play golf as well as taught him how to hunt and fish. He was always bringing him along with Scott. Did he do that things with John too? What was his motive behind engaging in that kind of behavior with John? because John was not his real son. He was the son he adopted.

When John was in trouble and was arrested, it seemed like the ideal time to get him out of the way and make amends for Jackie's history. In the end, I'd like for you to know what sort of a family dynamics there is in our family that's quite unhealthy. My guess is that this is not the ideal approach to raising children. Not.

Children who are emotionally and physically healthy However, we must continue. Then Scott received the majority of the spotlight, isn't he? Particularly following John was sent home as it's all about him and Scott was a man with very high standards. It was his duty to show his family pride because he was their only child left.

In essence, John disappeared. John isn't even a person we know now. He's in a completely different location. You have to continue our tradition. This is. You are the only one to blame. He seems to have handled the stress very well as well. Rose to the event. Scott Peterson was in the Cub Scouts as was his mother. She was the troop leader. The other parents and the troop say that they saw Scott as being a bit more different from the children.

He was extremely courteous. He was very kind, however he was discrete and preferring to just of be quiet. When their children were roaming about, just like typical six and seven years olds and stealing trees Scott was more inclined to be quiet. One thing people recall about Scott during the past, was his massive smile, the ease with which Scott would smile and how large his smile was, and how bright it was on the entire face of his.

As Scott was in fifth grade, his family upgraded their living area. Again, they were always striving to stay ahead of the Joneses. They actually purchased an extremely spacious and nice residence in Polo. There was a area in the backyard. It was a lovely, large backyard. Was surrounded by the Creek. This would make it an ideal spot for kids who were just starting to get older.

The student was selected by the teachers from the painted rock middle school for duty as a crossing guard between school and at night. This meant he was the child who would have wear an orange vest, and had to basically tell children not to cross the street as cars would soon be arriving and he was taking his duty extremely seriously.

And the people would get mad as the man wouldn't allow anyone to pass. Also, the cars were miles away, but he remained very careful. Yes. He would then say"hold on!. All the parents would become frustrated, and, you know, Jackie recalls a parent telling her"Come on, please don't let anyone run. When he was in his teens, Scott worked at a country club situated in Rancho Santa Fe, and there was a lot of time at the club, taking golf lessons in off days and learning how to improve his swing as well as his game on the golf course.

It's true that Lee Peterson was very proud of his son's his natural talent in golf. In my opinion, Lee is probably not an inherent talent in golf, since you've had to put an iron into the palm of his hand. He might be able to walk. But regardless, he recognized potential in him. And he stated that he made an agreement to purchase his son an expensive Ferrari.

If he can play at par. He's now an avid golfer. It's not me, I find it extremely boring. But I don't exactly what the term "par" means. It's not clear if this is impossible to accomplish. The only thing I can think of is Scott truly wanted the Ferrari. Okay. He snorted in order to take a shot. When 16 He was given keys to the car.

The dad fulfilled his pledge however, it was not an Ferrari. It was smaller, less costly and suitable car for the 16-year old no matter. He was given a car due to his golf skills at high school. He was named golf team's MVP. Twice. For the most part his classmates, he was remembered by the other students for being a simple, pleasant man.

He was seen wearing polo shirts as well as Letterman jackets. Yeah. He might have been a bit pompous, but he wasn't any more so than the average student in high school wearing the polo shirt as well as Letterman jackets. The coach for golf at high school recalled him for having a very nice manner. Never swearing, not using bad language and always able to control his feelings.

Like the other golfers well, yeah. Players on the team they'd shoot poorly and they'd toss their clubs and yell to the heavens and run into the next hole. On the side of the coach, when Scott who might have shot poorly did not react, he simply went to the next hole and then shot another. He did not show emotion. He did not show any anger.

He was always calm and in the right place after graduating. He was awarded a scholarship to participate in golf at Arizona state college, but it was only a single semester. It's been reported that he had a bad time at the school. The boy got one of the students playing golf in troubles for drinking and partying which led to him being ordered to quit, however I'm not certain if this is real because I didn't locate it.

Chapter 2: The Information Is Confirmed By Several Sources However

He did quit after a semester, and returned to California. He was a student at Questo college it's a local college. He was also a student at the university of Abispo and was there for a little over one year, before moving to another college. He then enrolled at California Polytechnic state university, where he earned a degree in the field of agricultural business.

He had an apartment style bachelor pad with his friends. They constructed fake grass on the flat roof. This allowed them to all walk up the roof to enjoy a beer and put golf balls in an adjacent field. The professors in Cal Poly. They all everyone loved his professors. People said that he was smart, intelligent.

He was very polite. One of his instructors advised me to be interested in taking a class that was full of Scott. Peterson's. As a student was working for himself, as well as paid for fees by working at various job. He was employed at a few golf clubs and country clubs and also in a cafe called the Pacific Cafe in moral Bay.

That's where the two met. gorgeous, bubbly brunette Lacey sent him a message. Lacy was full of enthusiasm in the light and enthusiasm, all wrapped with a 5 foot single frame, with dark locks dark eyes and an erect smile that was incredible. It could have been a small thing. If I wanted a shorter, she was 3 inches smaller than me. And I believe I'm tall But she was definitely robust.

She was determined. She didn't fear everything. Her mom Sharon says she remembers Alyse was such a great child since the very beginning. Two days later, her return from the hospital, that she started sleeping all night. My daughter is now two and a half. She hasn't changed since she was little and she was able to learn growing things and also to cultivate, and she spent lots of dollars time in the garden with her mother gardening as well as learning everything about plants and flowers, and the ways to help things expand and live.

The family had the dairy farm and Lacey found herself very at home within the farm. She helped by putting manure in the pond and Milky her cows. as well as her brother Brent could just be found spending time searching for ways to keep them busy at the farm. It was very enjoyable because there was always a new exciting adventure.

She said that at the very least that he was a huge movie buff and that she watched the same films she was a fan of time and again. As if she never got bored of them, particularly Superman. Her favorite was Superman and her mom told her she was. It was almost fun watching these kinds of movies together with Lacey repeatedly as Lacey would respond in a way that made it seem like she was watching it for the very first time she was laughing.

As if she'd never watched the movie prior to it. When something occurred that left her feeling angry or frightened she would cry. Even though she'd seen the film fifteen or twenty times. Sharon was required to show the films that Lacey would be watching because she'd be so angry and emotional over what appeared to be even the most insignificant thing.

It reminds me of so very much of Aden. The same thing happens in films. He isn't able to watch Mulana for a while because her father was a wrathful obnoxious time and she was able to break into the hunchback Notre dam. You can forget about the incident. It's not a film ever in the future. I forced him to watch it once since it was one of my all-time favorite Disney films as a kid.

He was there when the Modo, the Modo was coming to the bell tower to celebrate the celebration of fools, all the people were wearing masks and dancing the crowd was jolly. Then they started to unmask the man and began throwing objects at him and harassing him. Like throwing fruit and food on him. Aiden was not a fan of an emotional crisis.

Like she was crying. He felt like reaching for the remote control to turn it off. He couldn't bear the thought of it hurting his insides so much. I'll just mention the children who are sensitive when they're around 6/7/8 and feel a sense of horror whenever they witness someone who is being victimized. These are the children who become the most powerful social justice fighters.

Do not encourage this kind of behavior from your kids. Because I'm sure people have done it, especially boys. Sharon along with her husband Dennis Roshe split up when their children were just beginning to grow and the divorce was difficult for Lacey as well as her brother Brent However, they were able to become closer due to the divorce. It's quite common in which children go through divorced parents, that they develop bonds that are stronger because they rely on one another and depend on each other.

Even in the latter moments, after Lacey disappeared it was clear that her brother Brent truly loved her and loved her, and concerned about her. The family lived together with Sharon and her family in Modesto, California, but they'd still return on the farm every weekend and spend time with their father.

Brent recalls Lacy frequently wanted to spend time with him. The thing about the other friends were, she was not a problem because he loved her. They had a close relationship. When she turned 13-14 and he began to realize it wasn't a good decision because his peers would always say to him that you're really adorable and he'd say"Nope, Nope.

Lacy was the typical jolly teenage girl in high school. She was an active cheerleader. She was part of a tight-knit group of her friends. They attended sporting occasions together at the school. There were sleepovers during which they would drink champagne when their parents fell asleep, only to end up having a hangover the next day.

Friends have described her as lively and energetic. She was bubbly and flirty. The girl never went between high school and college. Her studies were in ornamental horticulture in Cal Poly and ornamental Horticulture is actually a research of growing effectively in a variety of flowering plants with a pleasing manner, perhaps as a decorative purpose.

You would expect someone similar to this appear as an event coordinator or florist, or wedding planner, or even a caterer, or some such thing. It says something about the character of Lacey. Her mother told her that Lacey was destined to be an housewife. She was a naturally-born homewife. Not all of us have the same qualities as the same as. I promise you.

She was a great cook. She enjoyed decorating her house to make it appear appealing. She enjoyed caring for others. She was a fan of entertaining, and inviting people over for dinner and cooking tasty food that people could savor. Yeah. While in the college years, she seemed much more mature than the average college girl. Her brother was close to her and the state and even after she was in college. Her father frequently drove to her home in order to see her in the school.

Then he told him that instead of inviting him to keg-party parties She was taking him to tastings of wines. He was well-educated. He knew what the things she wanted from the future. She recognized what she stood for. She didn't have to search for her in the living room or a fraternity, while she was working on an ice Keg Stand. You, she was more sophisticated. She had a mature appearance and didn't.

I felt like she was forced to spend her time performing activities that were not likely to lead anywhere. Scott and Lacey's path interacted as she ate lunch at the café which he employed. She may have spotted him in the distance, and saw the way he interacted with others with his smile and big smile the way he was charmed by everyone.

Since he was in the business of tips, and Lisa actually handed her contact number to a colleague of hers, who was working there and told him, you know that you should you can give it to the guy. Another employee Lisa's friend offered it to Scott and Scott tossed it away. Initially, Scott thought that it was a prank. It was true that he had seen her and believed she was gorgeous.

He believed that she was way outside his realm and thought they had played a game against him. But she returned to the café and was asking him, basically, know, she's an easy-going person. She asked"Why don't you contact me? I'll call you back with my number. They began to date immediately after that. In the meantime, Lacey was calling her mother Sharon prior to when they'd had their first meeting.

Then she told her, "Listen mother, I've already had a conversation with the man I'm planning to get married. The only thing you need to do is get there as soon as possible and get to meet him. Then Sharon said"Well, have you ever go on your first date? Then Lacey told her yes, but we'll. The couple did meet for their first date in the same week. Scott did Lacy deep-sea fishing it was something Scott was extremely attracted to, from his early years and also spending time with his dad who encouraged his interests on Scott.

However, Lacey isn't so sure. This is why it irks me this way, it's a strange dynamic. Was it because Scott have this knowledge through his dad? In order to get with someone, you must be able to make them feel similar things to what you like or else they'd be difficult to have around, or was he simply wanting to be a show-off to Lacey to say Hey I'm the one with these eyebrows Hobbes glance at me far better.

The first day could have included perhaps an evening meal and a movie. relax, eat an evening meal together chat with her, discover the kinds of activities that she enjoys doing. Find out what she's interested in and perhaps you're interested too. You've taken to deep sea fishing with her during a first date, where she'd be on the water for all time. It was seasick in the boat as she isn't a fan of vessels and might have said to you that she isn't a fan of vessels.

You would've been wise to not taken the girl on a date and maybe I'm thinking about it too much. Sharon Rocha drove down to see her daughter's school over the weekend, following the first time LeSean and Scott had a date. Sharon along with Lisi were able to eat breakfast at the Pacific café at which Scott employed and had already set up the table for him.

Two dozen roses were in the dining room, including 12 red roses for Lacy as well as 12 white roses for Sharon. Scott recognized how crucial Lacey's family was for her. Scott knew how much value Lisi placed. in the unit of family and within her own family. Therefore, he was being clever. If he was looking to get an endorsement for his new romance from his mother of the family, he needed to get the attention of her.

Every mother will appreciate seeing her daughter being courted, served and drank to the max. Also, to get flowers of your own and he's even including yourself instead of giving your daughter a shower. Yeah. This is going to be a great way make the mother feel special and that it did. Every person who met the couple back in their early years could not be more pleased with how about how in love they were.

They were together for all of their time and were together for two years prior to when Scott made the decision to propose. They were married in a stunning ceremony outdoors, with over 150 of their most beloved family and friends. Two months prior to the date Lacey left the college. From a distance it seemed like they would be the ideal match two attractive individuals who were happy and smiling well-educated, outgoing and determined to live their lives the way they wanted.After college, the pair set off on a journey together which led to them starting a the business industry with each other. They transformed an old-fashioned bakery that was located in a strip-mall to a restaurant known as"the shack. The idea was to turn it into an area for nearby college students to visit to on weekends to socialize and have some food and drinks. Scott made use of the experience was gained while working in the Pacific cafe in order to receive discount on food, and also to purchase used kitchen appliances.

Lacy employed her interior and exterior design expertise to transform this place into one that is. Modern, and also chic sort of space. Peanuts were everywhere on the tables, and she changed an older wine barrel to be exact. into a garbage bin. Her cool, hand painted signboards of driftwood. There was a fishing box which was hung on the front of the building.

It was a awesome location. It became a famous college hangout the two had hoped it would become. Both were successful entrepreneurs. They were both young. had just graduated from college, and were about to open the first restaurant. They were taking on a venture that was difficult. In reality, 9 of 10 establishments do not survive one year. However, they had faith of themselves.

It was a partnership. They worked in tandem. Then, Scott could not find any nearby people who could install the events, he realized that they would need to be able to pass the inspection. Scott went to LA and was issued the certificate he required to put in the vent by himself. Additionally, Lacey was a perfect hostess. Scott stated that they have already had a blast having dinner in their homes.

She was a cook. The family loved grilling. They enjoyed having guests to visit and the owner said, why don't we start an eatery where we could perform all of that. There is plenty we enjoy doing already and are money for it. In 2000, the couple have sold their busy and profitable eateries for profit and a substantial amount.

Then they made the decision to move to Modesto which is where Lacey was born. The time was time to have a baby. The kids had been having fun. They'd gone to university, they'd owned an establishment.

There were nights spent having fun and drinking and, now Lisi was really looking forward to. to start the family. There's a possibility that Scott was not keen about this idea, and he'd have put it back for a few years, because did not really want children. However, Lacey was.

Then they began to explore moving to Modesto was a dream of Lacey. The family she was with was also there. The group she had made up of her students from high school was present. She believed it was the ideal location to have a family that had family members who are welcoming and supportive of them. The couple bought an apartment in the neighborhood of Covina Avenue at a cost of $177,000.

Scott was employed by an Spanish agricultural supply firm known as trade Corp as their West coast representative for the West coast. The clients he worked with consisted of major farmers and flower farmers from Arizona, California, and New

Mexico. In addition, because he was selling to customers as well as a variety of diverse States and States, he was often required to travel, and leave into town or away from the city for several days due to reasons of work.

Lacy was hired as a substitute instructor, however, her primary goal was to make the house into a place to call home and a house suitable for her husband she adored and her children whom she was sure she would enjoy. The garden was planted out in the open and installed the pool and fence for the backyard.

Scott was a member of a local country club. Lacey was known to have dinner dates with her classmates who were in high school. They lived was an extremely good lifestyle. They appeared to be happy. All was well. All was in order. proper way. The Petersons were expecting their first child. A boy called Connor, Connor Peterson.

His room was decorated with an all-white and blue nautical theme. It's tragic considering what could be the outcome and how he could be. The holiday season was here in Modesto as well as at the Peterson home. Lacey decorated the home to celebrate Christmas. In between the prenatal visit and classes at Lamaze along with her husband Scott The day preceding Christmas Eve. This was an ordinary day for Lacey as well as Scott.

Chapter 3: Lacey Is A Half-Sister Named Amy's

Also, they have the same father. However, they do not the identical mother. Additionally, Amy is 6 years older than Lacey. Amy actually worked at an salon for hair located in Modesto where Scott and Lacey were able to go for their hair cut. On the day prior to Christmas Eve they went to see Amy on the evening of Christmas Eve to receive Scott's hair cut.

Amy did her usual shift the previous day. She then also left the salon in order to visit a local market or farmer's market to get fruit baskets will present to their grandfathers at Christmas. She ordered the various items she was looking for in the basket. They were then going put together the basket, and the person who was to return on the next day between the hours of 12 and 3 at night, after which they would collect the basket that day. It was the night before Christmas, and she returned to her salon.

Scott and Lacey are waiting in line for her, and she set her down and cut Scott's hair. While she was cutting Scott's hair she chatted with Lacey about the plans coming up tomorrow. She mentioned she needed to pick the basket between the hours of 12 and 3. Then, Scott said he'd take it for her.

He told me that I'm planning to go out. I'm scheduled to play golf today. That's why I'm headed that in the morning regardless. Then I'll get it for you. Also, Amy felt relieved as she had to work again, an entire shift the following day's work, between six 30 to 2:30 pm. Therefore, she wasn't going to cut the basket until she would not be able to reach the basket.

Since she needed to get home from early for work and this would just save her from a long trip. She was happy to accept his invitation to assist. Amy claims Lacey was dressed in a black shirt and a cream-colored flower in the top. The outfit was a cream Capri pants, dark jacket and a cream scarf.

Following Amy was done with Scott's hair. Lacey would like to know how she could dress her hair in such a manner that it flips over at the end.

Then, it was that Amy bought an iron to curl as well as a flat iron, and attempted to teach Lacey how to do it. They were amused and laughing about this. Scott later invited Amy to come over to dinner. Scott said that they planned for pizza, and then play football. He was asking if Amy wanted to attend. However, Amy claimed she already had plans.

Then she was passed over for the rest of her life. It will be the word of Scott Peterson. According to him, when they left the salon, around 630, the couple stopped for an order of pizza while driving to home. Once they arrived at home, they took their pizza, and then watched the Monday night football. After that, they are ready to sleep and put on their pajamas.

Lacy was wearing Scott's blue pajama bottoms. They got in bed, and were watching a movie while in bed. After that, the rookie the two went to sleep. It would've taken place around 1130. The family believes they fell in bed. The night of 23rd December eight thirty, Lacey made a call to her mom, confirming the that Christmas Eve dinner was scheduled to be served the following night since they would enjoy Christmas Eve dinner together with her parents.

Then we are in the early morning hours day of 24th. Scott claims that Lacey started her day around 7:45 am. She dressed. She put on her blue pajama bottoms which were worn in the evening before going to bed to the hamper, where they were discovered by police in the morning. She went down to eat some cereal. Scott advised her take a bite as shortly as she woke due to the fact that she was expecting.

In the event that she didn't take her food in the first few minutes after she woke up, she'd be nauseated. Scott was up at eight at night and walked downstairs to eat breakfast cereal. Lacey was with him as she was eating a slice of toast. Scott was planning to go golfing on that particular day. He took a shower while dressing, Lacey talked with him about what she was planning to do.

That day. The baker was preparing an French toast recipe for brunch on Christmas morning. she realized that the bread needed to be soaked in the egg mixture for some time in the range of eight to twenty hours. It must be kept in the ag mix before baking it. Then she decided to go to the grocery store the same day Christmas Eve day so she could purchase the items she required for her French toast cake.

Then she could make a marinade for the bread. This recipe for French toast baked thing was on the counter in the Peterson's house. The woman also said that she wanted to take the dog for a walk the day before, their pet McKenzie. She took walks with McKenzie every day. This is how she kept herself active during her pregnancy. She also said that she planned to sweep the flooring.

Also, make gingerbread cookies. Scott. Ben mentions that he observed Lacey at the bathroom and she was sitting on a stool that she brought to the bathroom since she had swelling in her legs as well as her feet due to pregnancy. Therefore, she would like to lie in her chair while she did her makeup and hair. Then he noticed her on the bench and was trying at flipping her hair over and make it look more stylish.

The way the sister showed her that night. When Scott spoke to him, in order about Lisa's mother's story, he told her Lisa was there as he considered, what a cute girl as she sits on the bench? Are you trying to pull her hair? The reason why this timeframe is crucial is that the following day Scott was to be charged with murdering Lacey at the time of her death on 23rd day of December. The prosecution would be so insistent in proving the prosecution believed Scott Peterson had killed Lacy Peterson on 23rd December.

There are all sorts of things going on early in the morning, when I tell you that the recipe was sitting on the counter, indicating she was planning to bake an French toast baked. Her pajama pant that were taken off, which were worn the night prior or were in the hamper. This is believed to support that the scout was innocent or at least, that the girl wasn't killed by him on 23rd.

But I'm not convinced that she was murdered on 23rd. The police arrived the following day, they'd find them of people in the bathroom like the man said. the curling iron of Lacey was sitting in the sink in the bathroom. The iron was unplugged, but the plug seemed to be extended and reaching for the outlet, which would be over the toilet.

They now have a housekeeper, who was probably there every week. The housekeeper claimed she'd visited just the day prior. The bathroom was empty. There wasn't a bunch of towels in the bathroom, and there wasn't a curling iron sitting on the counter. Then, Scott says he loaded three large patio umbrellas in the rear of his pickup truck.

The owner wanted to transport the umbrellas to his warehouse shop. The neighbor was actually watching the umbrellas being loaded into his truck. He waved to her. She waved back and said good morning. He seemed to be in good spirits. However, there are reports that suggest he might have been putting these umbrellas with a lot of other things on the truck.

None of these claims or sightings can be confirmed. Scott returned to his home and filled up the mop bucket to Lacie. To allow her to mop the floor of the kitchen. Then he claims the show she watched was Martha Stewart at the time and it was her most-loved show. When he was getting ready to go out the house, it was reported that Martha Stewart mentioned something about Moraine or merengue, or something similar.

When Lacy started mopping her floor Scott took her hand and kissed goodbye. Scott left the home between 930 and 10:10 morning. However, here's a question. If there was a maid or a housekeeper that had only been there for a day prior, then why would Lisi be cleaning the floor? In the morning, if the maid or the housekeeper were present or the housekeeper were present prior to the date it, why did the housekeeper clean the floor?

Was Lacey simply a neat person? If so, I'm sure of extremely meticulous about what she did to maintain her home, which was exactly how Shannon Watts was as well. I've always was curious about what it was like that Shanana Watts managed to keep her home tidy and clean even with two children, as I can't seem to manage it. However, Lacey was very meticulous about how her home was maintained.

It was extremely tidy. It was well-organized. Perhaps she was just cleaning daily on the floor. It's just not something is known for certain the extent to which she performed. It's just speculation for now. Okay. A number of people, such as Nancy, grace, who was extremely open on the Peterson matter, believe it's bizarre the fact that Scott left his expecting wife for fishing or golfing, or whatever else he ended having to do at the end of Christmas Eve.

Personally, I do not believe this is an advertisement to me. this is ad-agency to me due to the fact that I have children. If my friends wanted to go golfing or fishing at Christmas, I'd say that's not the best time to enjoy time with your youngsters. If we were married and had no kids, then yes. If we were just my husband and me, we weren't parents and it was just us. My husband also wanted to golf.

Christmas Eve is a holiday for me, and I be fine with it as I am sure we have plenty to accomplish, so it's much easier to let him away from the home in the middle of it all without distracting me. When you have children, and Christmas Eve can be a bit chaotic in the family atmosphere, however throughout the day at Christmas Eve, just before they went to dinner with the family in their home I have no issue about Scott playing golf or fishing or just doing something to entertain him.

It's not my opinion. She was expecting. Sure, she was pregnant. But she was also an adult woman. She didn't require to be supervised by her partner. The husband didn't have to be at home to watch her be sure that she didn't the idea of eating the cran, or peek her eyes out. It took nine minutes to journey away from the Peterson residence to the Warehouse.

That's the gap Peterson that he rented for storage of his boat. It also serves as an office. When the time the phone was in his car, records indicate that when he checked his voicemail, it was 10,088, and received a message from the boss. When he arrived at the warehouse, and then logged in to the computer, where he can to check his emails.

Chapter 4: The Dog Is Seized

The email was also sent to his boss with reference to the voice message. The voicemail was heard by him in his car. the evidence is documented in the records. It is clear that the employee did check his email and that and checked his email and to find the voicemail which he then sent to his boss. It is all verified. He was, therefore, in his storage facility.

Then he Googled directions for assembling the woodworking tools it was just delivered on December 20, through the post. Then there's about a 20-minute time interval during which Scott's location or where his activities are during the time that he shut off his computer. When he went out of the building, the tool for woodworking that He had just searched for directions on how to put together was completely completed.

It is therefore appropriate to suggest. It is possible that he was making that up in the twenty minute time frame. He was also able to get the roll-up door inside the warehouse. His vehicle, or truck was in the garage while the boat was within. Then he began to take tools off his truck to the warehouse. The report says that at the moment the man reached inside his toolbox and injured his finger with an instrument. it was bleeding. There was blood that was found at the entrance of his car.

It's fascinating because each time you hear about a warehouse, such as Scott Peterson had a warehouse that I envision this enormous large, massive, space with tall ceilings that simply huge. However, this was a warehouse and in reality, not large enough. It was was more a smaller garage, or perhaps one of those storage units.

Centers are like Storage Wars. There are these rooms. Then storage spaces are available within the rooms. This was more of that dimension. It was big enough to accommodate the boat, and also an office desk or computer. This was not a huge space even in the slightest. There wouldn't have been enough room to drive his vehicle into the warehouse to hook the vessel up. Instead, he was required to drive his vehicle closer to the Rowley doors that were was able to open and attach his boat to the dock just like that.

The boat was in the inside while there was a truck outside, and they would be connected before pulling the boat away. For those who believe that Lacy's body was thrown inside the boat via the truck while it was inside the warehouse, he'd need to have done this and then move her body out of the truck. to the boat in full sunlight.

Therefore, I'm unsure of what the level of traffic at that mall was. There might have been other shops which were operating, or when the doors to his store was in the direction of different businesses. It's a thing to consider that I had no idea about beforehand. I've always thought of it as an even bigger warehouse in which he could move the truck around and accomplish whatever it was he needed to do and then get it out, without anyone being any wiser.

Berkeley Marina Berkeley Marina was one of these. Marina's located on San Francisco Bay and it's just 90 minutes away of Scott's home. When he's in the house of his warehouse. A neighbor of Peterson's, Karen service, she observes the dog McKenzie strolling through the neighborhood walking around with the collar and leash that is still in its collar.

She also knows the dog. She has a good idea of the Peterson's. The dog is seized and then she finds McKenzie at the back of the home of Peterson's and shuts the Gates. So McKenzie, can't get back out. Scott Peterson gets to the Marina and has an entry ticket to show that the Marina was where he had parked. He also has an official launch certificate to prove the boat's launch from the marina.

This is the proof of his presence in this Marina at the time of his comment and he also says that it was North approximately two miles prior to when finding himself on the small Island with an inscription on it which read Nolan. Also, there was litter and rubbish on the Island and some broken the piers. The man thought that was a suitable area, shallow to attempt to fish.

You could say that's what you're doing. I'm not certain if that's an expression used in fishing or troll, but it's a term that can be used to describe a. The man decided to trolling in the area. Then he set up his anchor according to reports, then began exploring the vicinity. This Island was later discovered out was a Brook's Island. It is believed that he wasn't in the place he claimed the island was Brooks Island, because he was able to explain the Island and how it appeared like, and the location it was, and all the stuff.

According Scott Scott the man who was responsible for his water lures, a stinger which he had just bought in the back of his truck. The package of lures for saltwater was discovered in the truck bag exactly as the bag he'd claimed it to be. Then he utilized an ice jig from the summit found in his tackle box despite the fact that San Francisco Bay is obviously saltwater.

The guy says he was trolling for a short time until he got damp, and then nothing seemed to be going on. The fish didn't seem to be catching anything. He decided to return for the Marina. As I mentioned, the police were later able to locate bags with new Laura's inside Scott's vehicle. According to him, they also discovered one of his fishing poles inside the boat.

There was a cost tag for the fish pool at the lower part of his vessel. He just bought this fishing pole on 20th December. A lot of individuals make this claim as if it's possible that it was really him out fishing, or perhaps he purchased an angler's pole. About four days ago, he placed it on the boat to make it appear as if it appears as that he had been fishing.

This is more likely to me, since the fact that he's a fishing enthusiast, or if he's someone who loves fishing and has there was already an angler's pole which he required for fishing on San Francisco Bay, When Scott returned to the Marina He claims there were a couple of people who ask him about his experience. For instance, what was the fishing going?

Then he spoke with them briefly. These witnesses, or the individuals he talked to did not get confirmed. He also mentioned that there were some maintenance personnel nearby enjoying a laugh when he tried to pull the trailer to the boat in order to hook it to the boat again.

They did claim to have seen an individual who was similar to his description having a hard time getting their boat connected. The truck was also there at the time. Let me be a bit quiet and say I don't believe it ever was a matter of debate as to which Scott was on his boat on that particular day. It was more of a question whether or not he set out with the intention of going out to fish. I'd guess that he was on that particular day.

I completely believe that however, I don't believe he went out on the fishing boat. His family members claim that Scott has been a fervent fishing enthusiast since the age of a child however, that does not really reveal anything about Scott Peterson in adulthood, being a scout in the fishing industry and adolescence wasn't as common. Actually, the fishing boat he used on that day was one he bought it on the 9th.

The cash was used. It was probably $1400 in cash. The price was similar to a an aluminum 14-foot vessel. Also, the previous time the owner had a year long fishing permit was in 1994. Today, you can purchase two-day passes. What's the difference between a two-day pass as well as an annual pass is two-day passes are about eleven to twelve dollars. While the year pass will cost you 30 dollars.

Therefore, if someone plans to go fishing more than say, once per year, it's likely to be on a year-long vacation because they're likely to earn the difference in money. But Scott was not going to go fishing at least once every year. It's not like he's one of the best fishermen. Additionally. This is perhaps one of the most interesting and intriguing item of evidence that we've discussed so far.

We can discuss the future. The man did possess an official fishing license. However, it was a 2-day fishing license. He was required to apply for in advance. Then he had provide dates for what to place on the license. He had also applied for a fishing permit with a date of Dec 24th, and Dec 25th ahead of time.

Then he got it when fishing the next day. He buys an inflatable boat on the 9th of December. He purchases a fishing rod on the 20th of December. At some point in between these two dates the applicant is granted a fishing permit between December 24th and 25th, allowing him to get fishing for about an hour or approximately an hour and half.

Does that sound reasonable? This is because here's the issue. Scott has told everyone they were going to golf in the morning, even though Lacey was unable to reach the very first few individuals he had spoken to. telling them that he'd played golf on that particular day. Yeah. According to him, once it was time to get back to his store, he noticed that it was freezing cold, and decided to change his mind. had just purchased this boat and wanted to take out on the sea and observe what was happening out on the water.How suddenly did this happen? vessel on the boat trip of Ben. If you'd had to apply to get a fishing license on this particular date prior to the time and I'm sure you have it's that reason why he's the one who is most responsible of everything. According to the Lacy family members, they did not be aware that Scott purchased the boat.

It was a hidden boat and nobody thought Lacey had any idea about it. There were even scats on dad. Lee Peterson didn't know that Scott bought an expensive boat. Lee claimed that it was normal to Scott to make huge purchases such as this, and then to not reveal the purchase to anyone and nobody even knew that the boat was his.

Allegedly. The boat was secret which he kept in his garage. It was not known to anyone. Then he informed everyone that they were going to golf during the day. He was not fishing. Scott claimed that he was at sea for approximately 90 minutes prior to Scott's departure time in the Marina. Also, at the time when his cellphone shows his departure from the Marina there was a total of an hour and a half.

That's 78 minutes for you to reach at the Marina park, have the boat connected to the truck and car and then, you know, put it into the water and get it out to where you're heading. You'll be left with is 20 minutes. Fish without having the proper gear to fish as well as saltwater with the wrong boat to use for saltwater fishing or fishing.

Because that boat was a freshwater vessel. This doesn't seem to make sense. This is it. Two minutes later He calls Lacy cell phone, and sends this text message. Okay, beautiful. You won't be able to develop farms in order to make this basket for Papa. I was hoping that you'd be able to read this and get to the field. I'll catch you up soon.

Sweetie. I love you. Bye. The driver stops at 325 and contacts Lacey's number again at 352, however there is no voicemail. It is believed that time documents from the bank prove that he purchased guests during time time 325. While he was studying, he did. Then he went to the Chevron station located in Livermore in which he had guests. and his warehouse located in Modesto The drive could take about 48 minutes.

He claims he was back in his workplace around four fifteen. He claims he stayed into the building for around five minutes. Then it was when he received a fax to one of his suppliers stating that the shipment was on its way and he recalled being dissatisfied. The shaman didn't intend to arrive sooner than anticipated. Then he was that room for long enough to read the message.

The facts were received by his fax machine at around 1138. Thus, it could have been transmitted at the time of delivery to his warehouse. Okay. When he'd gone to the Marina. Therefore, he'd have noticed it upon returning. That's why that's the case.

Then it is basically that he removes the boat from his truck, then puts it back in the warehouse closes the large roly doors, and leaves the middle of I'm trans, and then gets into his vehicle and heads back home.

He claims he was home at around 430 or four 45. He then said in the evening, and at it was that time. It makes sense when you consider the place he was from and the things he was up to. After he returned at home, he discovered that the Landrover owned by Lacey was sitting on the driveway. He assumed she was at home. When he got inside the room, he realized that she wasn't in the house, however her purse, keys, along with all of her belongings were still in her possession.

Then he noticed the fact that McKenzie The dog was playing in the yard along with Leshawn. Then he walked out into the backyard. He took off the leash the dog and brought the dog inside and later he saw the mop bucket in the same spot as the time Lisi was mopping the floor, according to reports. Then he emptied it after which he thought that he wanted to be cleaned for the Christmas dinner on Christmas Eve.

He washed his clothes and put them into the machine to wash. Okay. Many individuals think that it's untrue. The man washed his clothing immediately after he came back home. This is among my things that I find not suspect, but it's due to my. Reference point. Scott states that he dealt in a variety of chemical and other things in his workplace frequently. Also, Scott knew that he had one of his wives who was expecting at the home.

Therefore, he'd always go to his home and clean his clothes immediately. To ensure that nothing was exposed to chemicals that were in his clothing and washed them separate. To avoid contaminating his other clothing by exposing it to things found on his clothes Therefore, when Scott came home and realized Lacey was not there and he wasn't sure if she wasn't there, that she'd gone or had disappeared or if something else was wrong with her.

He assumed her mother was picking her up and taken her home to help in the Christmas Eve meal earlier I think He didn't seem to be acting strangely, doing nothing but rambling about. His day got home. His clothes were soaked after a day of outside. The smell was probably a bit strong and he needed to clean them. Then he put them in the washing machine and put them in the dryer and washer were on the top floor of the house.

He didn't need to walk upstairs to put his clothes. The right place was there. My husband is the exact identical kind of thing. He's usually in the garage fixing his car. And after that he'll walk in and take off his clothes before entering the home. Okay. Then he puts them into the washing machine, usually all by themselves.

Just clean them prior to getting in the shower. It's a nightmare. Since I'm always asking myself would you've put any of the other 5 million objects placed in your hamper exactly in this approach and possibly made this the largest load. It's true that people don't often think that way. It doesn't appear strange to me that he washed his clothing like it was a way to remove the evidence.

It is possible that he was washing his clothes in order to rid himself of the evidence. But at the at the same time I believe Scott Peterson was a little OCD. When he returned home, they were dumped out from buckets. He didn't want them just lying around. The same thing that my husband would've done. The man is extremely OCB. He is quick to wash his clothes.

Similar to what my husband is doing. Also, he's very OCD. The cops who came to check on Scott Scout, he was extremely concerned about them. He would park in the driveway, then open their doors, possibly scratching his vehicle. My husband park in the opposite end. From the parking lot. This means that nobody park the vicinity of his vehicle.

Then he becomes angry when other cars park near his car regardless of the fact that he was parked in a different area from everyone else. It's my opinion that most likely, deliberately did this to annoy me because you're insane. Additionally, when the cops came in Scott's house and were conversing with Scott, he was constantly getting coasters to put in their drink.

It seems like he might have been somewhat OCD. This doesn't appear to be out of character to the guy. It's something my husband has done often time. This seems to be normal to me. However, it's my personal perception. My point of reference. After throwing his clothing in the washing machine and commences the process and grabs a pizza. He has the pizza container left from the night before at the counter.

Then he grabs a slice of pizza and began eating it. He and then pours himself a glass milk and goes upstairs with the milk and pizza to shower. Once he's out of the shower it's time to dress. When he returns downstairs, his eyes are caught flashing on an answering machine. This indicates that there's unheard messages there.

He presses play, and Here's his text message for Lacey earlier. Then he gets a call from Lacey's stepfather. Ron grand ski called earlier that morning to ask the possibility of LeSean Scott bringing whip cream for them at the time they were having dinner later that evening, as they ran out of whipped cream, and needed it to bake the desserts.

This is the time when Scott began to think"Hmm. If she's not here, she's not there. What is she doing. Then he called the house of Sharon as Ron and Sharon responded. Then Scott inquired what was your daughter's relationship in your home at all? Then Sharon replied, "No. Scott's saying, well it's true that she's not in the area. Her car is there and her belongings are here.

Now Sharon is going to say she heard Scott stated that she immediately was absent. Lacy's missing. It always seemed with a strange question: why in the event that you'ven't had a conversation with your wife for over one hour, do you be quick to say that she's missing Scott says? He has never stated that, but or even that he wasn't in the wrong, but his car was present but she wasn't. He did not know where she was, therefore, at this point Sharon suggests that to go find her.

We'll call the hospitals, and then call her family members. Scott walks out in the community, writes McKenzie walking on leash and then starts searching for Lacey thinking that maybe she fell and got injured. and knocking on doors of neighbor's. This is when neighbors actually took McKenzie from the backyard.

Ask Scott about what transpired when Lacey hid McKenzie in the back yard at 10:30. That's why Scott could have a frame of reference to conclude which was that Lacey has probably been missing since the time she disappeared at 1030 in the morning. It was like just when he was leaving to go into the store. Her parents have been making calls to her family and friends, everyone who could be related to them, and calling hospitals as I mentioned, and then they get scared and Ron is like"I'm going to contact the police and make a report Lecy missing.

Nine One One in the evening, around 5:47. Is this the call? Hey, could I aid you? My brother was in law. He fell and was injured. He was golfing. My daughter was not doing anything. Today, she is 8 months pregnant. The dog went for walk, walking with her. Dog returned with this shot of belief and came back with the daughter.

Who is your name? The name I use is Ron.
I'm doing work for the conductor. Okay.
What's your name? K Y or

her husband was a theater goer.

Your step-daughter.

Chapter 5: He's Black, White, Hispanic, Asian

What time will you pay me part? Then come back and say we're not sure. Just received a phone call from my son-in-law and he said he went out today at 9:30 and the ball was played about an hour and a half ago. He was and was not around. He went for a walk with his dog. Take a walk to win and you'll find the park. It's a mobile home park. is the park that's over there.

Again, a lot of people find it odd or bizarre to think that Scott wasn't the only one to announce Lacy missing. In this instance I'm not sure. Scott was in the area with his dog looking for Lacey, Ron and Sharon had returned home, feeling lost but were able to contact people and check what they might be able to tell.

It makes sense they'd be the ones to dial nine the other. It's important to remember that it wasn't days and weeks following the time she was absent. He knew she had disappeared. Scott returned home sometime between 4 30 and 4 45. She was discovered missing by Ron at 547. This is a total of an hour or an hour and fifteen minutes in the top tier.

There's no way Scott realized she had been missing for a few days, or days and did not call police. Someone was thinking, he should contact the police to report her missing. As if we should take action like he did. He's sure filed a missing report. It's not a issue. As he got home after searching for her following the fact that Ron was notified of her disappearance The police spotted Scott Peterson and Sharon and Ron as well as Lacey's buddies who all came out in support of each other as well as to search for her.

They all met in East LA Lomas park. This was the place in which Lacy was known to take McKenzie to when walking. Therefore, they decided this would be a great starting point, particularly when they heard from a neighbor of the fact that McKenzie was found along together with Alicia at around 1030 They all believed that the police were aware that an incident had occurred to Lacey during her visit to the park.

The helicopters were sent out in order to look over the park before dawn and get a better idea of look. If the woman was in there or if she fell or was pushed out, the entire neighborhood was looking for her. All the neighborhood members was out at the night of Christmas. The entire neighborhood gathered on Christmas Eve to search for the girl that everyone have become attached to. Everyone knew her from the area.

The woman was very friendly. It was her first pregnancy. People were concerned about her. Thus, tons and tons of people rushed out to assist. When the helicopters are searching at parks for Lacey The police then are asking Scott to investigate his house. Scott says yes there's no problem. It was incredibly cooperative from the gecko, and also oddly tranquil.

A calm and relaxed person, not as one might think someone whose pregnant wife was gone would act extremely Chris Watson fish, just playing with punches, and just going along with the rhythm. If you were in need of to contact him you needed him for, he was there however, he didn't seem to be frightened. What about where's my wife? Where is my wife. The woman is pregnant and we have a child.

There is a chance that she could be in any place. She may be injured. It is possible that she will pass out. How do you know if she has beginning to laboring and couldn't find assistance. What's the problem? Her stuff is all here. You're worried, your wife, and the baby are not there. There's a chance they're in a place where she put her things in this house. Also, you're probably wondering why she wasn't even a bit less worried, however it wasn't the case even.

That's what caused him to be a target for the police initially. Detective Albert Keeney was one of the very first police officers to be involved in the Peterson investigation. The detective went through the Peterson residence on Christmas Eve to determine what was out in the normal, or not in or out of. Then he replied, "No It didn't look like that. The home was clean, well-maintained extremely tidy.

The man did not notice something, and that was that the bed Lacey was making that morning was perfectly made. Like my husband, probably. the beds perfectly using corner corners in hospitals, similar to my method of making them simply by covering the blankets with pillows. They were perfectly made, but there were two small indentions on the base of the bed. They were on the comforter, which seemed like someone could be sitting.

Then they went through for the Scouts for the death of one fifty and the Lacey's home Rover. They didn't find any items in the area. What they did find inside Scott's vehicle was two patio umbrellas as well as an Tarp. This is my query. Scott was putting the patio umbrellas and patio furniture in his pickup truck the previous morning, to transport them to the warehouse to be stored there.

Why are they there? They're still inside his truck the next day. He's been out and about back to his warehouse. He isn't aware of taking his umbrellas off. Perhaps the umbrellas on his patio were simply a cover for hiding. That was on the back of his pickup truck. Burkini will also conduct a brief inspection of Scott's warehouse however, Scott informs him that the power is off.

Therefore, the burkini needed to shine his flashlight, and he glanced around at the area to determine if something looked odd or perhaps she was in the area. Then he didn't notice anything. Then he went home, but the next day he called the power provider to find out what time the power was restored in the complex or inside the warehouse. This allowed him to return to get a closer look as well as the electricity.

Then he said power had was never out there. There have been no reports of power outages in the area whatsoever. L bro Kini was a bit puzzled to see Skadden are so concerned about the disappearance of his wife. Also, he determined to establish the date clear. We've had Scott arrive to interview. This wasn't an interrogation.

He claims the interview was in which he chose the date However, something was different concerning Scott and the entire situation. Unsettled, a bit of a burkini. Then we switched to the tape recorder something he wouldn't normally be doing during an interview with the spouse of a person who is missing I'm sorry, brother Keeney and ask Scott some questions. that he wants to know, for example, could be you tested to see if there is gunshot residue?

Scott's response is, yes obviously, he's got hands that are placed over his in this moment for Keeney finds the cut is fresh in his finger. Then Scott states, yes I cut my finger this morning. As I reached for my toolbox. In the end, I took whatever was out of Scott Peterson's hand. This day, it was not examined for gunshot residue.

In the end, I'm not sure what the purpose was. However, burkini is asking God to let him be able to pass a polygraph exam and Scott is like I'll. I'm tired tonight, and I'm anxious. That's why I want to get home, but I'll go to work the next day. We've set up a polygraph test to be taken the following day. Scott was also asked regarding his marriage.

Are you in a happy union? Did you and your spouse have problems? Did you fight? And Scott says"yes, it was a great union. There was no difficulties. There was never any fights. All was well. The following day, Christmas Day about 30 minutes before the

the scout was supposed to be taken to the police station to take his polygraph. He contacts.

He says that he have talked to my dad. It's not an ideal concept. We're not planning to take the polygraph test. What do you consider and should you, in the event that your spouse went missing. If they were murdered Would you pass the polygraph test? Since I'm aware that they advise that they don't because polygraph tests are not research-based and can be inconsistent with their findings.

If the police suspect you of a crime, they ask you to take this test and say you're lying However, it reveals that you're lying. There could be more evidence to pursue you however the findings of the test aren't legal before a judge. The reason is this, because they're not actually.

True. I've always thought that taking an examination with a polygraph revealed more about the innocence of your subject rather than the actual results. However, I'm not sure whether I'd take an examination with a polygraph. If my husband had gone missing. or killed because I believe it's their method of getting you to feel apprehensive and then using that to harass you.

They'll then bring it back. The result will be similar to how that you didn't pass the polygraph. We've seen this happen when we saw West Memphis three, like that you didn't pass the polygraph. What is your secret? You're guilty. They may make use of it against you. Therefore, I'm not sure whether I. Consider it a given however, What do you think? Please let me know. The press picked up the heart of the matter on the 26th of December.

In essence it was the media were camped before Peterson's house Peterson house for all day and night, but they stayed. The time was when 24-hour coverage of the media in the TV news was on and it was common for broadcasters to conduct things similar to this in order to fill up the gap and try to cover all hours of coverage.

Then they'd get video of Scott being out walking Scott, his dog Scott receiving post, Scott taking his vehicle. Then they would be present every time. It was something I thought could be a big snub particularly if you were innocent, and the wife of your partner was absent. However, for some reason Scott did not talk to the media at all and everyone thought it was odd because normally a loved one of the family members or spouses of a person who is missing should be before the camera whenever they can to spread the word and to draw attention to the person who is missing, to plead with the person who has their attention to find them.

For them to return to them, please. However, he didn't intend to take part in the camera. He was not interested in having pictures made of his face. He'd always be out with sunglasses on with a hat, and to turn his back towards cameras and attempt to keep his photo from being on the internet at all. In the meantime the neighbors as well as people living within the area were being interrogated and there was a lot of accounts of witnesses who claimed to have seen Lacy strolling her dog the morning of December 24 There were at most 12 accounts of those who observed Lacy.

However, only three were followed-up with the only contact being phone calls. They were never met in the flesh. The reason why these reports are crucial is due to the fact that when people see Lacy taking her dog for a walk after nine thirty in the morning and it was proven that Scott was headed to his storage facility, as it was, then he could not be accountable for her disappearance or the murder that followed.

Many people believe that police didn't care about the reports. and didn't pursue the reports because they were concentrated to Scott as being the individual who was responsible. They were convinced of this, they thought they weren't required to put any trust in the people who saw Lacy the day she was murdered.

Here's an image aid below, showing the blue dot that is where the Peterson home. The red dots represent the locations which Lacey was discovered that morning. There was doubt at one time that these sightings might be from a different woman expecting within the same region. But it was not Lacey even a bit.

The woman, who also walked her golden retriever each and every day, in the same area chemotherapy, the woman that gave birth in the month of October. In December, she would be no longer pregnant. She also says that she's 99.9 percent certain that she was not out on Christmas Eve. If she did been out walking in the morning, she wasn't more pregnant. Homer Maldonado States that he observed Lacy strolling her dog.

Between 945 and 10:15 am on the morning of Christmas Eve. It was just 1/2 mile away of The Peterson home. The man claims he slowed down to have a closer glance, which was creepy. Why are you slowed down for a great image of? He says it's because he remembered the fact that she was pregnant. Homer affirms repeatedly that it could not have been anyone else but Lacey Peterson.

He reported the incident to police on January 1 and was not pursued by Vivian Mitchell who lives roughly 10 blocks from Peterson's. The woman also said she observed Lacey in the morning, out walking with her dog. Vivian claims she is certain that it was Lacey due to the fact that the couple previously seen Lacey on the walk before.

And Lacey was stunning. It's impossible to duplicate her beauty. It's impossible to find someone who you could not mistaken for Lacey Peterson. The woman reported it to police, too. They gave her a phone call three weeks later, and after that nothing. The 26th of December, Albrook Keeney returns to the Peterson home. He takes with him a person who, if they called him as a backup plan, a second investigator identified as John Bueller.At the moment there is a suspicion of scats, and there are many reasons to the suspicion. One reason is that the case that when someone dies or disappears in nine out of ten cases, it's their spouse or someone that is very close to their family or friends. They also thought it odd it was that Scott was willing to sign the polygraph only to get from it after a minimal time.

In general his manner of appearing so cool, serene and calm didn't go to how one would act when they're expecting a wife is missing.

Then they returned to meet with him. to ask if they could inspect the house once more, they asked him, would you agree to let us visit and take a look around the house once more?

Then he replied, I'm fine I'm fine, but please stay with me. Call my lawyer to verify. Police claim that they entered the house and demanded to check inside the house He immediately refused and that he did not think this was a good decision. But, Scott says he told them"yes," he didn't think about it. Scott was planning to contact his lawyer.

The lawyer then took the money for a long time to get his money back and police became impatient. The police pulled out the warrants and said"We already have a warrant in place to check your home and automobiles and storage facility. It's just a matter of seeing what you'd say. Please, step back. What I discovered is that Scott just two days after his wife went missing He has already gotten his lawyer involved.

To me, that seems like a suspicious situation. It's likely that he was aware that they believed they were suspects in this. Perhaps he was seeking to be ahead of the situation. They also took both of their vehicles along to test. They removed Scott's F150 as well as Lacey's Land Rover. They also took the boat from his storage facility as well as inspected his storage facility.

Police department organized a press event to question anyone who is public. Anyone who might have seen the scaps truck? Then they displayed images of Scott's truck. Then they asked If you've witnessed this at or in the vicinity in the Berkeley Marina, okay. Tell us about it. Because we're trying to build the truth of the matter. The group was saying, okay do you think Scott Peterson a suspect right this moment?

The police also said that it's not possible to discuss that in the moment. Therefore, everyone now believes about Scott Peterson is a suspect and that's not getting an overwhelmingly positive reaction from the public all over the world. The media is quick to start pursuing Scott's parents and him as well. The parents of Lacey were there to defend him. The mother of Lacey said If you were to know Scott and the love he had for my daughter, you would not be witnessing this happening to Scott.

They haven't heard anyone speak a word of anger against one another. I've not heard them argue. They've also never had them say a nasty or negative word or anyone other. They formed a team. They were a happy couple. They knew for certain of the fact that Scott wasn't involved in anything that occurred to Lacey.

On December 30, however there was a flurry of events that could cause everyone to be thrown into a spin. The young lady named Amber Frye contacted police. They asked her if she was in an affair with Scott Peterson for over a month and that he not told her that the fact that he was married. What happened when Scott and Amber were introduced is a romantic fairytale that will last for a lifetime.

Scott was visiting Fresno on business and was staying in an hotel. In the bar of the hotel Scott began to smack the woman in the bar questioning her about what she's most favorite sexual position was. The woman was in shock"Whoa, slow down and cowboy. I'm with a woman already but I'm sure of who you could enjoy and you think Scott could like this woman was trying to introduce him to was her closest acquaintance, Amber Fry.

Let me know how did you set your favorite acquaintance with that unsettling guy in the bar that tried to pounce upon you using a pick-up question of what your most preferred sexual position is? Amber was a

27-year aged massage therapist in Fresno along with her 2 year old daughter. Her life was single and was looking for someone to share her life to and provide her with an element of security.

The friend of hers set the date for her on an uninitiated date with Scott Peterson and, after Scott arrived at Ambrose door, he was waiting to whisk her out on the first time and she said she was amazed at how friendly and charming. Also, she says that I found it adorable because he was not nervous. He explained that he'd experienced anxiety in his stomach as he made the way to get her up.

The plan was to have dinner however, Scott told them, "Oh you know, I've been at work throughout the day. I'd like to change off of my clothes and into new clothes and be nice for you, and clean up. Let's stop to my lodging. It's really fast. That's why I could get freshly conditioned when they returned into his hotel room. Scott was already setting the table with a champagne bottle as well as chilling red roses as they celebrated their bright future and growing romance.

It's true I find it impossible to believe the girl was at the moment, you can see that the guy you met was an agressor, isn't he. You are a creep, or only had a conversation with him. Before he's even invited the dinner table He's waiting for you to be inside the hotel room. After they had a glass of champagne they ate dinner together and after that, they hung out at a Karaoke bar where they performed an duet, and then they slowed danced till the bar shut at.

After that, they went back to Scott's hotel room, where Amber was staying the night. telling her that she was single and was seeking the perfect one to share his life with. He stated that he was looking for an intimate relationship but the interest was not to have children. She was perfectly content to have an infant. He was not averse, however the fact was that he did not want children that were his own.

He was simply overloaded. He had a lot of work to do. He left town all the time. Amber was a 27-year young woman who hadn't experienced much luck with regards to romance. One time she was with an older man who was married, which didn't work out. Then she was pregnant with a different man who broke up with her after the latter found out that she was expecting.

Then she became all alone, a single mom trying to take care of her daughter. She enrolled herself in school and became an acupuncturist and was looking for a partner who could share her passion with and bring some stability to her daily life. Her daughter's life. Scott was charming and handsome. He was charming. He presented her with roses.

He said he felt the feeling of butterflies as his time to collect her up. He had done a great job. She figured, you might have some money. He appeared to be a complete package and she couldn't even think about why things were moving as fast as it was. I think. The first time they met was the 20th of November, and they continued to stay connected.

They spoke on the telephone a lot, however the man told her that he was in Sacramento and she resided in Fresno. Therefore, they didn't get to see one another often. From November through the close of their romance the couple only physically visited her only a few times however, they talked over the phone almost every day.

He went back to Fresno to visit Amber on the 2nd of December. He also went with Amber and her daughter for a hike and brought the two back to his home, where he cooked their dinner. It's an amazing story. Chris Watts to me, just right. 100% correct. A double life. It's true, the most significant difference is Nicole Kessinger was aware that Chris was married. But Chris told her that they were separated from their wife.

Chapter 6: While Scott First Told Amber

That they'd never had a wedding in the first place, the 9th of December was changed. He called her and said he had something crucial to share with her. Would he be able to come over? He went over to her home and dropped the bomb at the door. He was able to say, I've not fully sincere to you.

I was married. the day I got married, my spouse died on the very day on December 9th prior to going to Amber's home to inform her that Scott lost his wife. He also and bought his secret boat. We know for certain that Scott was not lost his wife. What does losing your wife refer to? A normal person would understand this to mean your wife died.

Right. This is what Amber did the incident. That's the reason she didn't bother on him any further for details as he claimed that it was painful to discuss in a fresh way. He was unable to do it. It was impossible for him to accomplish it. We're aware that Lacey was alive in December 9th, but she didn't seem to be very alive the 14th of December the day that Scott came back in Fresno carrying three dozen red roses. and he was a lover of his flowers. He she was greeted with champagne, and the couple took a sip of champagne.

He then invited her to an event for Christmas. The same night, Lacey attended a Christmas celebration in Modesto all by herself, Amber asked Scott Peterson to trust him without hesitation? Scott Peterson said yes. Scott replied, I'm sure you are aware that the answer is completely ambiguous. Right? It's extremely vague. He's like doing the whole generalized, vague concept rather than saying I'm sure you can trust my word with all your heart.

He's trying to not be a liar. It's the way a lie is done. Liars don't like to openly declare something that could then be used against the next day. Therefore, he claims that he have lost my spouse. He doesn't say my wife died. He doesn't tell me that my wife and me got divorced. He doesn't mention that I'm planning to murder my wife. He states, I've have lost my wife.

This could refer to any thing. Right. If she came back and said I was thinking that you had claimed you were divorced from your wife. You could argue that I really lost her. It's like we had a separation emotionally. So I felt. Like she died. I felt like I'd lost her. She asked me if I could be sure to trust you with all my heart? Then he replies, "Yes I have the answer.

The man is so ambiguous. It's not like he has a purpose however, it's still a bit hazy. So scummy. was at Ambers for the night, then the next morning it was announced that he would have to go home and head to Maine to work. He was also going to travel across Europe to job. Therefore, he was only able to meet her for long and then he told her"When I return.

I'll answer any question that you may have and be discussing this more in the near future. It's so shocking. It's my first Christmas I'm spending with my spouse. It's too difficult to think about it this moment. However, after the holiday season, when I return from my trip I will be talking about this because I love the people around me.

Amber was able to ask Scott the address he resided at or if he has an address to deliver a Christmas gift to him, since they didn't meet during the holiday season. Scott also provided her with an address to mail a letter that was located in Modesto, California. Yeah. This made her think since he said his home was in Sacramento. What is the reason you own the PO box located in Modesto?

The 23rd of December, Scott was in the presence of his wife. It was the final entire day in the time she lived. Scott phoned Amber and informed her that they were in Maine duck hunting along with his father.

Amber did not get a call from him until the 24th of April or on the 25th. However, on the 26th she got in touch with him. He told her his flight would be to Paris in the morning. But she wanted to make a call and leave a nice message for his voicemail.

Anyway. However, she was so shocked by the way he walked up to her. Right. He should be in a plane, he should not have been able take his cell cellphone. She asked"Where are you?" He replied, I'm living in New York. She said shouldn't you travel on a plane? Did you missed the plane? Was it a glitch?

He was like yes, that's what I'm supposed be. However, she's saying What, how did you not inform me that you were living in New York? In the event that you did not fly to Paris? Why wouldn't you contact me? Why would you not inform me that you're in New York? What's happening? What did he do was that it was under the watch of the police at the time.

They seemed like they were over his head and, well that he might not have felt at ease calling you, and perhaps you thought he was in the news. But Amber was not able to notice him in the news. The news wasn't on her radar. She had no idea. Yeah. Was there anything going on following that whole I'm actually here in New York, but I said I'd be in Paris matter, however I'm in fact.

Just here In California. It's not too distant from where you are. Amber begins to become more sceptical. That little uneasy feeling that has been telling her for several days there was something wrong began becoming more. She decided to call an acquaintance of hers who was a cop working for that department. Fresno Police Department.

Then she didn't look into Scott. It might sound odd for some in the world However, I believe it's amazing. You know, you shouldn't lie to women. If you're not willing to call our cop buddies to check on your background, she thought her friend will call back to say that he's got a wife but he's sorry. However, she was not prepared for to hear anything about her acquaintance, police officer, or Fresno after he contacted her at one hour early in the morning on the 29th of December.

He also gave her an address and phone number. He said that she should contact this number to speak to them. The phone number was the department of police.

2 INSIDE THE CASE

The police were just able to discover the identity of a lady known as Amber Frye, who had been involved in an affair with Scott for several months.

and Scott has told her prior to the time Lacey disappeared, that he'd been widowed. Prior to the police becoming aware of Amber and her disappearance, they began investigating other possibilities apart from Scat. Naturally, they were concerned about that scats were involved. The man was husband to the woman not found. Most often, the motivation behind an act of crime like it was a result of someone near to the victim However, they did look for other possible motives.

Right. If anyone in the vicinity were recently paroled in connection with violent crime, mostly for women, was examined, spoken to and it was a long time since each of these persons was identified by police, as they spoke to, and then deemed suspected. Police sniffer dogs in order find the path of Lacy at dawn on 24 December, however they kept chasing them across the highway, as did the dog's handler of the dogs was not able to stop them.

They explained that it means Lacey was not leaving on foot. She was in a car. Another tip was brought from. Just opposite Peterson's house The Medinas as well as the Medinas were gone during Christmas. After they returned the next day, they discovered that their home was broken in the entrance.

Was kicked out of the safe that was not there and a few other belongings from the house. They called the police and filed a report. Police immediately started investigating the crime. Then they discovered another neighbour to the Peters. Diane Jackson said she was passing through the Medina house in the 24th of April.

She noticed something which caused her to think for one more look. Look. The driver was moving very slowly since the area was residential and she saw one of the vans parked on the driveway of the Medina residence. There were two people sitting in the street. She was also driving at a snail's pace, she sort inclined her head to see them.

The two of them looked directly at her. It caused her a sort of weird sensation. There was something that did not feel quite right.

But, she didn't consider it after she learned that her family was robbed when the family was away on Christmas. Then she phoned the police and told them what she observed.

It is evident that if the crime occurred on the day of Christmas Eve morning The crime as well as Lacey's disappearance may be connected because she was absent on the morning of 24th. Did she interfere with the burglary? Do they know that her neighbours had gone out and say Hey, what're these guys up to?

They then grabbed her in order to keep her from revealing their identity or reporting their presence to police. The robbery may have occurred on the same day that she disappeared. This could be a link which needs to be investigated through. The police swiftly located and arrested the suspects that were involved in the robbery. Dave as well as Todd Wayne and Donald, Glen

Pierce. Glen Pierce were apprehended and interrogated.

The first thing they told the police during interrogation was there was nothing in connection in the disappearance of that pregnant woman. missing. They also said they had not taken the home in a burglary on Christmas day, however, on one day following Christmas, the 26th of December, Todd claimed he was in the location frequently. The house he saw was empty.

Perhaps he was in the process of kissing it and then he saw there was no one around. Then they went inside to break in to the property and removed the safe out, and then put it out on the lawn before going in to steal the remainder of the belongings. The police had an open press conference, and stated the robbers and thieves have been caught are in police custody, and have nothing to do with be associated with what transpired to Lacey Peterson.

Lacy Peterson went missing on the 24th, and the people were not within the area around Lacy Peterson's residence until 26th. This is why they're base their whole argument that the robbers had nothing to have anything to do with Lacy being missing based due to the fact that they're there within two days of her disappearance. missing.

Although I was there when they placing them on the 24th, police continue to push this account of what been a reality on the 26th. But the issue is that, as we all know that on the 26th of December of the 26th day it was reported that there were vans from the media and networks outside the Peterson house, attempting to get a look or be interviewed by Scott Peterson who was avoiding these vans like a scourge.

Ted Rowlands, a reporter working for KTV. It is reported that he was the front of the house. The other media outlets were reporting on December 26th around 5:00

am. They surely could have seen an armed robbery taking place in the home just across the street in particular if the thieves were to have taken the seat file and put it in the front line as they claim they did and Ted states that he's old.

He's searching for people that will get out of their homes since he would like to speak with them on their neighbors, the Petersons. Scott was not talking with the Petersons. The group was sat there every day, in anticipation of something happening. It's a difficult time thinking that a robbery may happen right before their eyes. They wouldn't be aware of it, or even try to talk with the victims who might have had neighbors.

Ted Roland says if he'd observed someone outside and he saw them, he'd rush towards them to attempt to secure an interview. It's difficult to imagine that the most shrewd of thieves will attempt to steal one of the houses right across from a circus. Actually, ever since Lacey disappeared and was never found, there was always kind of media or police were present outside the house.

This would need been happening on the 24th day before the woman went missing. Because nobody is going to cover a home just across from the woman who went missing? There are police officers and news vehicles all over town. No one's doing this. There's always someone out there that would have noticed something similar to this.

Why are police attempting to disengage from the Medina home, and also missing Lacey Peterson, Diane Jackson and Diane Jackson? The woman who witnessed the men questioning for the Medina home for help on the 24th of April, says that the police tried convincing them that they were wrong. They claimed she had mixed with men outside the Medina house with people who were in her yard during this week.

She also claims they tried to use hypnosis in order to persuade her to alter her story. But she did not do. Even to this day. To this day, police continue to adhere to their story. They tell the story that the robbery took place on 26th of June, I am not convinced was the case. I am of the opinion that normal common thieves would Rob an apartment and get into the act of kidnapping and killing pregnant women.

Actually, I don't even know them, so I'm not aware of their background was. In other words, I'm unsure the extent to which they were desperate. It's extremely difficult for me. As a police officer, having no access to the past of these people, being unable to speak with the men and assess their degree of financial desperation in the time.

It's difficult to figure out the actual capabilities they were skilled at. In the coming weeks, we'll get back to this robbery and the people who participated in with the nets, Scott Peterson's lawyer. They could have explained the reason for their presence and how they could have been tied to Lacey and other information to be revealed regarding these people later during the trial of this trial.

It's possible that there will be another part in the story. Therefore, I'm sorry to hear that you're frustrated by the numerous pieces and long components, but it certainly requires a part three. I'm thinking I've made a decision. The movie has three parts and we'll get returning to Amber Fry and how her mere existence led Scott Peterson to forever be blamed in the court of opinions of the people.

The moment Lacey was missing, police put up an anonymous tip line that allowed those to dial the police station to give their suggestions. It will then become the task of investigators who would determine which tips are worth being followed up with now. Albrook Keeney occurred to be within the vicinity in which this tip line was being conducted as he walked by.

The operators on the phone who have been taking tips. Then he heard one the phone operators talk to a person via the phone. He got a small glimpse of the conversations. He was standing behind her, and began listening to her and the words she was writing in her head. What she was typing was that this woman claims she's been contacted by Peterson's girlfriend.

They've been dating for about a month. Then he says"wait, hand me the number. He then rings with Amber. He says, Tell me all you know. Amber shares her story with Albert Kimi once more, and the man thinks, we've had Scott who is Scott, aren't we? Scott is there, and he's with a different woman. The wife of his partner is gone.

We now have an explanation, something that they had not prior to. He tells Amber"You are safe. Myself as well as John

Buehler were to come here and we're planning discuss things with you and settle this issue. Don't worry. They immediately go to her residence. Albert Piney and John Buehler were sitting alongside Amber and she shared with them all the details starting at the point she'd had a meeting with Scott up to the very end after she realized the real identity of Scott.

Yeah. Then they were told the story of how Scott was telling her on December 9 He had fallen in love with his wife. They said"Oh We've taken him. They've got him. It's over. Someone from outside may think, what's the matter, then is he looking at all? He tried to come clean with Amber. He came forward and was trying to explain that he was married.He was unsure of what to say. The man was still. Right. It's actually not the situation actually. Since the day preceding the 9th of December, before the date he shared with Amber. Amber's half-truth friend. One of the people who connected them, in fact reached out to Scott and asked"Hello, I've heard of you that you're married. I'm sure of what's happening.

If you don't inform her I'll give you a enjoy a wonderful to stay. Scott is off, buys the boat he has hidden in cash. He then visits his house with his girlfriend and shares her tale of how she was able to lose his wife. Branchini and Bueller inquire Amber Do you want to record the conversations you have with Scott? It's likely to be difficult not to come to him and challenge him about the details you have However, it's best to maintain it at a minimum and maintain this friendship as Scott continued to call Amber every single day.

We'd like to capture these conversations to determine if the man will give us something that could help in finding the missing Lacy or Connor. Also, Amber was scared at first but what was the point? Since at that point, she believed he was an icy blooded murderer, however, there was there was a baby absent, and she had enough guilt to be a part of the entire situation.

She also wanted us to do everything we could in order to help. The detectives took her to a radio shop. They purchased a recorder can be connected to the phone, and it will record. Conversations with the person calling when they're showing the user how to hook it onto her phone and how to use the. The call will ring.

And it's Scott Peterson. We're going to take a small part of the call for you today.

yeah.

The phone rang, it was on December 30, and Amber was required to answer it and pretend to not be aware that Scott was a professional criminal and a liar, or even a murderer. The phone made Amber very scared since she wasn't prepared. Her anxiety and fear were overwhelming. It was fortunate that Amber did not have to perform any doing at this time since the connection wasn't good.

Amber remembers shaking to the core. On that telephone call, she told her she felt she must maintain her momentum. She stated that she was certain that if she behaved differently she would be a different person and lose the possibility of being able to find the issue. LeSean Conner, she must get her acting ability improved, as within the next evening Scott was calling her a second time.

Today is the 31st of December A candlelight vigil taking place for Lacy and Connor in East LA Loma park. The event was attended by a large number of people praying each day for Lacy could be returned safe. As Lacy's family, and Scott's entire family took to the stage to express their gratitude to everyone who was there to stand with Lacey and to ask for prayers to pray for the safe return.

Scott remains hidden in the crowd. We thank you all for being here this evening. Lace you'd be thrilled to meet. Lacy had a lot of friends and admirers and you can't stop seeking out license plates in price. The mother of Lacy Sharon admits that she was aware she was at the party, however she never saw Lacy throughout the night.

Ah, they'll are asking you questions about the candlelight ceremony. The event will be held in a park. They asked you why you weren't on the stage with your family? In truth, the way we are conditioned to appear on camera we must strive to bring home that one person hurting. One of the most essential pieces of our family members is currently missing.

The media, however, did catch Scott. They were able to see him often and took pictures of him laughing, socializing and smiling. He looked more like a spectator at a sporting event rather as opposed to someone who has losing his wife who was pregnant and wasn't sure exactly where she was. Scott's sister-in-law claims that the reason Scott was smiling in several of these photos was due to him talking to his young niece, who was also in the midst of a baby.

And he smiled at her. It's not like he was trying to make her fear him and cry and be devastated. That's totally normal. In truth, the smile of the man in the photos isn't any reason to be suspicious. They looked awful when newspapers printed the photos later that day. But it was not my idea of being suspicious because there's plenty of people in support of the wife and you. They've been there to help your sake.

Yes, you're likely to be smiling at the people. They'll be patting you on the back. They'll talk to the person and it's not a an incredibly sassy thing at all. But what's suspicious, is when you pick up one of the phones with your girl friend at a candlelight celebration for your wife who is missing and some telling her you're looking forward to celebrating New Year's Eve in front of The Eiffel tower.

Chapter 7: Aluminum Wedge Of Aiud

In 1974, a piece of art with the form of wedge was found in the eastern part from Aiud, Romania, on the banks of the Mures River. The workers found the mastodon bones of prehistoric times and this aluminum wedge next to one another in the sand. The bones from the past have been discovered to be predated by approximately. 2.5 millennia ago. The wedge was reminiscent of the shape like the head the Hammer.

The relic from the past was delivered into the Archaeological Institute in Cluj-Napoca. The relic was measured and weighed at 5 Lbs and measured at 8x5x3. The wedge was covered with aluminum oxide which was then examined by experts concluding that it was between 300 and 400 years old. Amazingly, the date of the wedge made from aluminum is thought to be around 11,000 years old because of its association alongside bones.

In 1808, aluminum was first discovered however, it was not manufactured in an industrial scale until the year 1885. Some people believe that it's not an authentic artifact. Others, however, believe in the idea that alien life came to Earth hundreds of years ago and was responsible for producing this alloy. Based on scientific research, the alloy was found to be an extremely complicated piece of iron. It's composed of 12 distinct elements. Eighty percent of them are aluminum. The remaining elements being silicon, copper zinc, lead, zirconium, cadmium, tin cobalt, nickel, silver, bismuth, as well as trace quantities of gallium.

The most popular theories about this wedge called"the "Object of Aiud" are they could be the remains of a vessel that crashed close to the river. This could be a sign of the presence of aliens from the past. Perhaps it was the remains of an ancient flying machine that was created on our planet.

Many believe that it is something else, perhaps even an excavator from the present however, scientists continue to consider the

mystery of it.

Aluminum Wedge Of Aiud

Antikythera Mechanism

Antikythera is a tiny island located northwest of Crete as well as the for the site of the artifact discovered by divers who swam through the wreck of a ship in the year 1901. It was made of bronze that had been corroded, and was a complex mechanism that included several wheels and gears. Its casing indicated the year of manufacture was around the year 80 BC. It has been regarded as being among the most advanced mechanisms to emerge from the early world. The X-rays of the mechanism showed that it was an intricate arrangement of gears that were differential. The type of gearing mechanism wasn't discovered prior to 1575. It's fascinating to know the people who built it, as well as the way this technique was lost.

It was determined in the initial stages of research that it might be an astrolabe(astronomical instrument), or a type of astronomical clock. The dials and coalescence gears are a part that of an mechanical clock. The device may have served to indicate the position of moon and sun and possibly even the globe, which could have been used as the basis for a calendar. The calendar may have been used to calculate the positions of planets as well as meteorological phenomena. It is comprised of three big dials as well as 3 smaller ones. Some theories about its usage as a calendar that can be used for purposes other than it being a solar calendar, or a calendar that includes moon and sun eclipses of the past as well as future for the moon and the sun.

New research suggests that this amazing mechanism to in the first century BC. It is described as a complete product, one of the most impressive clockwork mechanisms with extremely precise equipment. The device was regarded as the basis of mythology in Roman as well as Greek writings, up until the discovery. The technology reveals a skills at an early level that has been lost through the generations. Some experts believe that it functions as a sophisticated mechanical system monitoring the periodicities in the solar system. Recent research suggests it could have been the very first computer that existed centuries ago intended to forecast the future of events. The modern-day version was constructed and tested, basing it on the original and was widely praised for being highly precise.

Antikythera Mechanism

Reproduction Of Antikythera Mechanism

Chapter 8: Baghdad Battery

An ancient battery of 2,000 years called the Baghdad Battery located in the vicinity of Baghdad in Khujut Rabu dating back to 248BC as well as 226 AD. The first discovery was made in 1936, and it is believed to be from the Mesopotamian region. The device was made of a clay vessel that had an asphalt stopper as well as iron rods that were enclosed with copper cylinders within the jar. It was in the event that it was filled with alkaline solutions, it could generate electric current. The intriguing object suggests they were aware of electricity, and the ways to generate and apply the power source.

The archaeologists found that the acidic liquid could create an electric charge in the container. Since there are no historic evidence regarding the time when they were batteries, what purpose did they make use of the charge? They were found with others similar jars. There are many who believe the ancient battery might have been used to electroplat objects with gold although no evidence has been discovered to prove this hypothesis.

Tests have been conducted with replicas of these batteries. They proved that they could be capable to produce electricity when filled with acidic liquid. The exact purpose behind them remain a mystery, and a method of production that has been lost. The discovery was made prior to the development of electrochemical cells, by using the voltaic pile during the 1800's, which was believed to be the work of Alessandro Volta.

Baghdad Battery

Copy Of Hieroglyph Of Ancient Electricity At Temple Of Dendera, Egypt

Carnac Stones

In the tiny village of Carnac with a population of five thousand inhabitants, in the province of Brittany located in northern

France There are 3,300 megalithic rocks. They are made of local rocks and were believed to be constructed by a small group of individuals who lived in the Neolithic time period between 4500BC and 3300BC. The standing stones of the prehistoric period have been arranged into perfect grids that are close to 1 mile in length and they're equally separated stones that range from to 1-4 meters in height. It is a mystery the reason why so many stones are arranged symmetrically within one particular area. they are arranged in patterns, whereas other stones are scattered.

There are various types of stones, one standing stone called menhirs and multi-stone collections known as dolmens. Two main stones aligned include the Menec alignment as well as that of the Kermario alignment. Additionally, there are other smaller alignments, known as Petit Menec. The Menec alignments comprise 12 simultaneous rows of menhirs and remnants of a stone circle each end. On the east side an alignment layout pattern is repeated into what's known as"the" Kermario alignment.

The reason for the stones have not been completely established, however many theories are being proposed. Some believe that the stones were placed in honor of their ancestral ancestors and use them to commemorate burials or other rituals of worship. Many believe that they're some kind of astronomical marking device that aligns to the solstice, or carrying out the function of a calendar, or they are employed in the detection of earthquakes. It is believed that each one represents an individual warrior from the Roman legion. They are changed into stone through the magic of Merlin . Therefore, there's no agreement on the real significance of these huge stones. In the present, some stones have been taken away from their initial locations since the people use them as building materials and for other constructions.

Mysterious Carnac Megaliths

The Carnac Stones Alignments

Chapter 9: The Crystal Skulls

The story of the crystal skulls predicts an time that will be a turning point in the history of mankind, in which the skulls of thirteen will be united, linking the wisdom of all holy planets and creating an organization of cognizant people from different worlds and attaining the maximum energy level possible in the earth's plane. Each skull is an archive of information that contains particular information. Once the skulls have been united and the 13th skull is placed at the heart of the structure, a new universe will arise through the extraction of all knowledge of the skulls. Humanity will then have to decide whether to utilize this knowledge for the good of us or to serve destruction.

The indigenous peoples believe that the skulls have extraordinary magical and therapeutic properties for healing. Some believe that skulls are able to manifest supernatural phenomena due to their powers of the supernatural and generate miraculous results. But, there's any scientific proof, derived in the research studies conducted of scientists that have confirmed this belief. There is no evidence that the skulls within the collections of museums were found through archaeological excavations that have been documented. Nobody knows exactly where they came or the purpose for which they came from.

The 13 skulls that are found all over the globe, and are part of the rituals and ceremonies which contain information on the origins of humanity as well as its civilisations. The skull carvings are made of white or clear quartz, believed to be Pre-Columbian Mesoamerican artifacts, believed to belong to Aztec and Maya civilizations. Crystals of this type, as analyzed through mineral enclosures can only be found within Madagascar and Brazil and is therefore not accessible in Pre-Columbian MesoAmerica. The study's conclusions are it was believed that skulls had been made during the 19th century in Germany. Some reports have suggested that the earliest origins of the skulls can be traced to the remains of the Aztec as well as Maya civilizations. Central America, South America and parts of Mexico.

A few people who believe in the skulls are real claim that the skulls are inhabited by spirits of the ancient Mayans that have entered the skulls in anticipation of the time that the ancient wisdom of their ancestors is required in the time of a crisis. The dates of the skulls could be ranging from 5,000 years up to 36,000 years old. This is way ahead of the civilizations which could use their materials. Quartz crystal isn't nearly as practical as obsidian which is plentiful and is used throughout the world.

Lasers are now utilized to sculpt materials. After numerous studies in the field as well as the latest electron microscopy analysis of skulls, it was discovered that both the

British Museum and the Smithsonian Institution skulls showed markings that were created using modern-day carving accessories. So, the researchers found that the skulls were not real and so are those that are in museums and private collections.

Believers in the legitimacy of skulls testify to the notion that the first skulls may have been substituted with fakes. Furthermore, marks do not mean that they are fake since many of the sites found have marks, drilling markings, or are hard to reproduce. This is why there's large debates in the scholarly field between spiritualists, scientists as well as archaeologists. All are trying to find out how skulls were made without breaking the entire object. Because whenever quartz or crystal is cut, it needs to be done using the direction of the rock and if you do not follow the axis, it can break into fragments. Who were these carvers and what was their ultimate goal with skulls?

Certain skulls may describe themselves as crystal clear with others are colored quartz, or smoky. Additionally, they could be of human-sized size, with stunning features, or be of a smaller dimension and less polished. The most well-known skull is the Mitchell Hedges in 1927. The skull was found in an old Mayan location in Belize. The smoky crystal skull of quartz was found during the site of excavations for the site of a Mayan temple. It was christened E.T. for its descriptive head that was shaped like an alien. The rose-colored quartz skull was discovered on the border between Honduras and Guatemala as well as the other skulls follow the same pattern as the Paris skulls.

Recently, researchers from The University of Southampton, in England have revealed that they are able to save and retrieve five-dimensional quartz crystal data. This is a first in terms of its the capacity of data storage, calibrating balances up to 1000 degrees Celsius and an almost indefinite life. It is an amazing discovery of the concept of a "portable memory" utilizing glass for the purpose of preserving humanity's past.

The Crystal Skulls

Nazca Lines

The well-known Nazca Lines, located in the desert around 200 miles to the south from Lima, Peru, provide huge geoglyphs of wildlife as well as spiders, insects, monkeys, sharks, as well as flowers. The lines are straight and include 800 as well as 70 animal and plant designs, as well as 300 geometric glyphs including the biggest glyph that spans 200 meters, and the largest glyph measuring 9 miles. The lines are perfectly precisely straight, while others are parallel and interspersed with the appearance of as if they were ancient runways for airports. The plain is 37 miles long and a mile wide thanks to these intricate patterns and lines. The lines have stood up to changing climate due to the absence of wind that causes erosion. temperatures range between 80 and 100 degrees in daytime but can drop down to 30 degrees in the evening.

They were first discovered in the second half of the 20th century, when planes flew across the desert, bringing food and other goods to the area. The Nazca Lines run between the cities that are located in Nazca and Palpa situated in the middle of Peru. They are believed to be the work of the Nazca people in the year 100 BC. They worked hard and constructed an underground system of Aqueducts to ensure an existence that was sustained in a desert climate. There were rituals of ceremonial worship in which they prayed for drinking water and for their crops to prosper. Then, the city was suddenly abandoned and there was little evidence of why they left their houses.

Researchers of researchers from the University of Dresden, in Germany are studying the lines, and have determined their magnetic field. They noticed variations on one of the lines near Nazca as well as conductivity of electrical current was directly measured in these lines. The results showed that conductivity of electricity was higher by 8000 times in the line than adjacent to them. This means that there exist distinct magnetic field anomalies situated about 8 feet under the lines. Radiocarbon dating, which was performed on these large drawings suggests they existed many years before the Nazca civilization. Scientists are unable to confirm their source or purpose with certainty.

There are many theories about the significance of these devices and their purpose. They are believed to be used to perform purposes of astronomy, such as monitoring the sun, constellations, and even calendar cycles. Some theories also include the use of ancient art as well as religious reasons, and an ancient method of communication between generations. The theory is that the lines are a reflection of the underground water supply sources within the area. There is a belief that they were created in order to create landing zones to UFOS or a different type of antique aircraft, taking the shape of runway markings. These lines and figures are in a proportional size which can be seen at an elevation of a certain height. This finding has baffled scientists since the 1930's as nobody is able to provide definitive proof.

Peru Nazca Lines

Monkey (The Nazca Lines)

Chapter 10: The Piri Reis Map

The original document, drawn in 1513 by the Ottoman Turkish admiral Piri Reis geographer and cartographer, was a map of the world derived upon the compilation of about 20 maps. Through notes about the map, he compiled and copied the information from these maps. ones that date from around the fourth century BC or prior. The map provides a precise geography that covers the American continent, with precision which is so accurate that certain scholars believe that it was a result in aerial photography. At that point of time there weren't any aircrafts on the earth as well as technology was largely restricted.

Piri Reis sketched an outline of the nearly inaccessible area in South America, notating rivers and lakes as well as mountains which were unexplored at the time in the past. The map he created depicted North Africa, the coast of Brazil and also the western shores of Europe. He also illustrated some of the Atlantic Islands such as the Canary Islands, and the Azores and even Japan. A mere third of the map is still in existence today. With the quality of the drawings shown, it's become the subject of much debate with the academics.

This archeological discovery was discovered in 1929 during the renovation of Topkapi Palace in Istanbul, Turkey. It was a worldwide attraction, because it is the sole replica of the world map from Christopher Columbus, and the sole map of the 16th century showing South America's accurate location in relation to Africa. Additionally, the map depicted the geographical features of Antarctica and mapped it before the ice covered it at the time it was free of ice. The Antarctica map showed the northern region being mapped prior to the cover of ice and the actual coastline being hidden beneath the frozen sea. This suggests the possibility that somebody knew, perhaps an elite civilization what the earth looked of years ago, from an airborne perspective.

There are many theories and speculations about various theories about Piri Reis map, with one being about who been able to access drones or aerial surveys which might have charted Antarctica in the past when there was no ice. There is a belief that ancient travellers traveled between poles and could have been exploring Antarctica Antarctic while the oceans were unfrozen, perhaps using a navigation instrument that was precise in determining the longitudes. A different theory suggests that the maps for The Piri Reis map may be traced back to the Minoans as well as Phoenicians who were skilled sailors during the early days of sailing. The source documents and charts might have been transferred, and then made accessible to Constantinople. The city has no definitive explanations for the exactness of this map or what it is that made it possible to create. The map is currently located inside the Library of the Topkapi Palace in Istanbul, Turkey.

The Piri Reis Map

The Piri Reis Map Antarctica

Taos Hum

It is believed that the Taos Hum mystery reports began in the late 1950's when the reports included an incessant high-pitched pulsation that was heard throughout the auditorium. The "Hum" occurred in specific zones, such as Bristol, England, Taos, Mexico, Bandi, Sydney as well as Windsor, Ontario. The ELF (extremely Low Frequency) sounds could be heard by around 2percent of the people living in areas that were hum-prone. They were more loud during the night and then began to diminish throughout the day. The investigation was conducted for potential causes, such as the events in the zone however, there was no any scientific reason to explain the noise.

Some people experienced nausea, headaches and suicidal tendencies since there were suicides during the 90's which were linked to this sound. There were complaints of a constant pounding beat, whining, unsettling sound that drove them to sleepless, restless days and depressive. The noise is detected through the naked ear is called the sound of a diesel engine idle as well as a myriad of other sound detection equipments are unable to detect it. Scientists confirm that there aren't any natural cause as the cause. It is not the result of a psychotic disorder or hypochondria.

There are a variety of possible theories for the cause of this noise, including wireless communications equipment, electromagnetic radiation electric lines, seismic activity or even military research. Most of these claims haven't been linked to mechanical or electrical reasons. In 1993, Congress requested to examine the cause of this problem. In 1997, they were appointed researchers and scientists to conduct studies regarding the noise. The initial findings confirmed the hum is abrupt and starts at a constant low frequency and there is a variation within the pulse. There is a possibility that it has connection to the technology used in military communications that is known as ELF. Infrasound could cause signs that resemble the noise of hum. It could be an auditory magnetism.

Theoretical theories have been suggested including alien communication or the sound produced by alignments between the planets. Some even believe that lost spirits could travel to another side. The Hum can be heard in the indoors but is also heard in rural areas. But the reality of the source of this noise, The Taos Hum, is a mystery of its origins and meaning are not yet known.

Depiction Of Taos Hum

New Mexico, Taos Hum

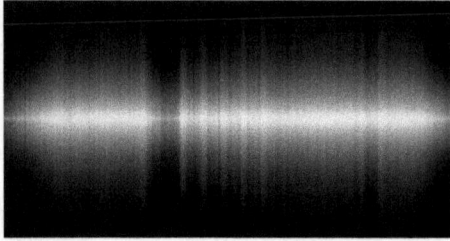

Chapter 11: Voynich Manuscript

The Voynich Manuscript was a long-standing document that was written in the 1400s in the beginning, written with a gazelle parchment skin with a language that was never read and not understood. It is a colorful collection of illustrations of plants, creatures and beautiful illustrations. It is approximately 240 pages long, and is divided into a set of paragraphs, which are illustrated and accompanied by diagrams and illustrations. Topics include the astronomical, cosmological, biochemical medicinal, herbal, as well as medical information. There are 20-30 glyphs, which comprise the bulk part of the texts. There's no evidence of corrections, errors or interruptions.

Carbon dating can be a clue to the script's writing between 1404-1438. However, there is no way to identify the name of the writer of the work. The manuscript was bought through an antiquarian book dealer called

Wilfrid Voynich, in the year 1912. It has been the subject of numerous unsuccessful attempts at decoding the book. The details of the book remain obscure, a variety of theories have been put forward to explain the book's true meaning. A lot of people believe it's an ancient pharmaceutical publication that depicts therapies for medicine. Some believe it's a sort of cosmological diagram, for instance, a chart of stars that was written by an extraterrestrial being. Many believe that it's an untruth, and is impossible to decipher.

The businessman of Finland, Viekko Latvala, who has made a public appearance and claimed to have deciphered the text and decoded its secret codes. He claims to be an "prophet of God". The author of the text was an astrologist who studied Astrology, pharmacy, astrology and also of plants. The writer studied plants to determine their medicinal or scientific purposes. Latvala says that nobody is able to decode it. It's an "channel language of prophecy." He asserts that the author's dialect was a distinct Babylonian dialect. He also claims that the sounds found in the text comprise a blend of Spanish as well as Italian. The author is believed to be the person who created his personal words. The manuscript text in the Voynich Manuscript can be found at the Beinecke Rare Book as well as the Beinecke Rare Book Manuscript Library. It is mysterious to this day.

Voynich Manuscript

"Wow"! Signal

The year 1977 was the time Jerry Ehman, a employee of the SETI Project(The Search for Extraterrestrial Intelligence) at the Ohio Wesleyan University's Perkins Observatory, was scanning radio waves that came from deep space at the time his observations reached their peak at a time that lasted for 72 minutes. It was believed to be coming in the Sagittarius constellation close to the star

Tau Sagittari located 120 light years from the earth. The signal was detected at precisely the right speed that it couldn't be considered to be noise and wouldn't be interrupted during its way.

Astonished, Ehman wrote the word "Wow"! on the printed sheet, which attracted a lot of publicity, and was later referred to for"the "Wow"! Signal. Every attempt to find this signal were unsuccessful. The meaning and origin of this signal has caused a lot of debate. Some believe that it could be our first contact with the extraterrestrials of an advanced civilization. In 2012, about 10.000 Twitter messages were broadcast towards the location the signal came from however, there was no communication.

The Center for Planetary Science, in 2016, proposed the idea that a comet's hydrogen cloud may have created"Wow" "Wow"! signal. They conducted 200 observation in the radio spectrum region from November 2016 and February 2017. Their findings revealed that the cometary spectrum can be detected at 1420 MHz. They also determined that the "Wow"! signal came from an "natural phenomenon from a solar system body."

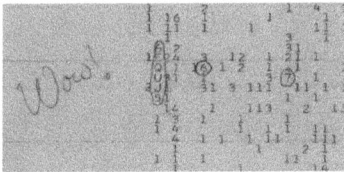

The "Wow"! Signal

The unsolved mystery that scientists, researchers as well as the most recent technological advancements have not been solved yet. The puzzles continue to surround these ancient discoveries as well as with our vast understanding of the civilizations there remain mysteries about which we have no answers. The book aims to provide insight into the mysteries, and if you enjoyed this book, I've produced a variety of ebooks about ancient discoveries.

They are titled The Ark of the Covenant: New Uncovering Discoveries, The Bermuda Triangle Unexplained disappearances Beneath the Waves, The Dead Sea Scrolls Ancient Secrets Unveiled Easter Island The Mystical "Stone Giants", The Shroud of Turin The Scientific Evidence, Stonehenge The Mysterious Megaliths And many more. Humanity will always be able to face the problems of the past and in the future by using their imagination and the power of technology to uncover the mysteries of the universe.

Chapter 12: Aluminum Wedge Of Aiud

In 1974, a piece of art that resembled an oval was found to the east in Aiud, Romania, on the banks of the Mures River. Workers discovered mastodon bones from the past and an aluminum wedge next to one another in the sand. These ancient bones were dating back to around. 2.5 millennia ago.The wedge had the look of the hammer's head.

The relic from the past was delivered by the archaeological institute at Cluj-Napoca. It was weighed and measured at 5 Lbs and measured at 8x5x3. It was covered by an oxide of aluminum which was then examined by experts believe it is at least 300-400 years old. It is awe-inspiring that the age of the wedge made from aluminum is thought to be around 11,000 years old as a result of its discovery in the bone.

The discovery of aluminum was made in 1808 however, it was not manufactured in an industrial scale until the year 1885. Some believe that it's not an authentic artifact. Others, however, believe in the idea that alien life was present in our world hundreds of years ago and was responsible for making this metal. After a thorough analysis, it was found to be a very intricate piece of steel. It's made up of 12 distinct elements. Eighty percent of them are aluminum with the other components being silicon, copper zinc, lead zirconium and tin and nickel. It also contains cobalt, silver, bismuth, as well as trace quantities of gallium.

The theories surrounding this wedge, also called"the "Object of Aiud" are they could be the remains of a vessel which had crashed close to the river. This could be a sign of visits by aliens in the past. It could also be part of an old flying machine that was created on the earth. Some believe it's something else, perhaps even it was a tool used by modern excavators but scientists are still unable to find the mystery of it.

Aluminum Wedge Of Aiud

Chapter 13: Antikythera Mechanism

Antikythera is a tiny island in the northwest region of Crete as well as the for the site of the artifact discovered by divers who swam through an accident in the year. It was made of bronze that had been corroded, and included a mechanism made up of several wheels and gears. Its casing indicated the date of its creation was 1980 BC. The discovery was regarded as among the most advanced mechanisms to emerge from the world of ancient times. The X-rays of the mechanism showed it to be a complicated arrangement of gears that were differential. This kind of structure for gears wasn't discovered prior to 1575. It's interesting to learn the person who designed it and the way this technique was lost.

It was determined in the initial stages of research that it might be an astrolabe(astronomical instrument), or a type of astronomical clock. The gears that coalesce and the dials are a part of an mechanical clock. The device may be utilized to present the position of moon and sun and possibly even the earth's position, in an astronomical calendar. The calendar may have been used to calculate locations of planets, as well as other meteorological phenomena. It has three dials, three of which are large and the smaller dials. Some theories about its usage for a practical calendar are one that is a solar calendar. an eclipse calendar that shows the cycles of the past and the future of the moon and the sun.

New research suggests that this amazing mechanism to in the first century BC. It is described as a complete product, one of the most impressive clockwork mechanisms with extremely precise equipment. The device was regarded as an untruth in Roman as well as Greek texts, prior to the discovery. The technology demonstrates a mastery at an early level that has been lost through the decades. Some experts believe that it functions as a complicated mechanical computer monitoring the cycles that make up the solar system. The latest research suggests that it might be the first computer in the past, which was created to predict in the near future what would happen. The modern-day version was constructed and tested based on the original and it was recognized as extremely precise.

Antikythera Mechanism

Reproduction Of Antikythera Mechanism

Chapter 14: Baghdad Battery

An ancient battery of 2,000 years called"the" Baghdad Battery, was found in the vicinity of Baghdad in Khujut Rabu dating back to 248 BC and 226 AD. It was discovered in the year 1936 and is believed to be from the Mesopotamian region. It was a clay vessel with an asphalt stopper and an iron rod encased by a copper-copper cylinder in the jar. When filled with alkaline solutions, it could generate electric current. The intriguing object suggests they were aware of electricity, and the methods to make and utilize electricity.

They concluded that the acidic liquid could create an electric charge in the Jar. There were no documents regarding the time when they were batteries, what purpose did they make use of the charge? They were found with different jars similar to these. Many believe that the battery could be used to electroplate objects with gold there is no evidence discovered to prove this hypothesis.

Tests have been conducted using replicas of the batteries. They proved that they could be capable of producing electricity when they were filled with acidic liquid. The exact purpose behind them remain a mystery, and a method of production that has been lost. The discovery was made prior to the development of the electrochemical cell and the voltaic pile around 1800, and was later attributed to Alessandro Volta.

Baghdad Battery

Copy Of Hieroglyph Of Ancient Electricity At Temple Of Dendera, Egypt

Chapter 15: Carnac Stones

In the tiny village of Carnac which is home to 5 000 inhabitants in the region of Brittany located in northern France there are 3,000 megalithic stone structures. They are made from local stone and believed to be constructed by a small group of individuals during the Neolithic period, which was between 4500BC and 3300BC. Standing stones from the Neolithic age are laid out in perfectly straight patterns that extend to nearly one mile long, and they're equally scattered stones that are ranging between 4 to 5 meters tall. It is a mystery how many stones can are arranged symmetrically within the same area, since they are arranged in patterns, whereas others are scattered.

There are a variety of types: individual standing stones referred to as menhirs, as well as multi-stone collections known as dolmens. Two main groups of alignments for stones are the Menec alignment, as well as Kermario alignment. Kermario alignment. There are smaller alignments that are called Petit Menec. The Menec alignments comprise 12 simultaneous rows of menhirs, as well as remnants of a circle made from stone at the ends. To the east an alignment layout pattern is repeated into"the Kermario alignment.

The intention behind the stones is not yet definitively established, but various theories are being proposed. Some believe that they were built to commemorate their ancestors they were used for burials or other religious events. Some believe they're a sort of astronomical mark that is aligned with the solstice date or the function of a calendar, or they are employed in seismic detection. The legend that is presented is that every form is an individual warrior from the Roman legion and was changed into a stone through the magic of Merlin . There isn't a agreement on the real significance of these huge stones. Nowadays, a few of the stones have been taken away from their former locations because they are being used as construction materials in homes and constructions.

Mysterious Carnac Megaliths

The Carnac Stones Alignments

Chapter 16: The Crystal Skulls

The myth of the crystal skulls hints at an time that will be a turning point in the history of mankind, where the 13 skulls will be united, linking the collective knowledge of all sacred planets, and creating an organization of cognizant people from every planet, achieving the most powerful energy that can be achieved on the planet. Each skull is an archive of information that contains particular information. Once the skulls have been united with the 13th one located in the middle of the group, a brand new universe will arise through the extraction of all knowledge of the skulls. Mankind will have to choose whether to utilize this knowledge for our benefit or harmful purposes.

Indigenous peoples believe that the skulls have extraordinary magical and rejuvenating healing qualities. Some believe that skulls are able to manifest supernatural phenomena due to their powers of the supernatural and generate supernatural effects. There is however not any evidence through the study of exhibits of scientists that have confirmed this belief. There is no evidence that the skulls in museum collections was discovered through excavations that were documented. Nobody knows which skulls came from, or what they were used for.

The skulls of these 13 are scattered throughout the world as a part of the rituals and ceremonies which contain information on the history of humankind as well as its civilisations. The skull carvings are made of white or clear quartz, believed to be Pre-Columbian Mesoamerican artifacts that are believed to be from Aztec as well as Maya civilizations. Crystals of this type, as that is studied by mineral enclosures are only available within Madagascar and Brazil and is therefore not accessible in Pre-Columbian MesoAmerica. The study's conclusions are they were created during the 19th century in Germany. There are reports that claim the earliest origins of the skulls are found in the remains of the Aztec as well as Maya civilizations. Central America, South America as well as parts of Mexico.

There are some who believe that the skulls to be real claim that the skulls are inhabited by spirits of the ancient Mayans that have entered the skulls in anticipation of the time that the ancient wisdom of their ancestors could be required during the time of an utterly devastating situation. The dates of the skulls could vary from 5,000 years ago up to 36,000 years, way ahead of the civilizations which could use their substance. Quartz crystal isn't nearly so practical as obsidian that is abundant and is used throughout the world.

Lasers are now utilized to modify the materials. In a variety of scientific studies and the most recent electron microscopic examination of skulls, it was discovered that both the British Museum and the

Smithsonian Institution skulls have markings which were created using modern-day carving tools. So, the researchers found that the skulls are counterfeit, just like the others that are in museums and private collections.

Believers in the legitimacy of the skulls support the idea that the original skulls might have been replaced with fakes. Additionally, the presence of markings does not make them fake since many ancient sites have marks, drilling marks and are extremely difficult to replicate. This is why there's a huge debate on the subject among spiritualists, scientists, as well as archaeologists. Everyone is trying to find out the method of carving skulls without breaking the whole piece. Because whenever quartz or crystal is cut, it needs to be done using the direction of the rock and if you do not follow it, it could break into fragments. What were the carvers who took their time and what was the purpose behind the skulls?

A few skulls could be described as crystal-clear, with other are colored quartz, or smoky. Additionally, they could be of human-sized size, with stunning features, or be of a smaller dimension and less polished. The most well-known and first skull is the Mitchell Hedges in 1927. The skull was found in an old Mayan site in Belize. An eerie quartz crystal skull was found during the site of excavations for an ancient Mayan temple. It was given the name E.T. for its striking skull that resembles an alien. The rose-colored quartz skull was found close to the borders of Honduras and Guatemala The other skulls follow the same pattern as the Paris skulls.

Recently, researchers from Southampton University, in England. University of Southampton, in England discovered that they are able to save and retrieve five-dimensional information from quartz crystals. This is a first in terms of its the capacity of data storage, calibrating balances up to 1000 degrees Centigrade, and a nearly indefinite life. This is an incredible discovery of the concept of a "portable memory" utilizing glass that allows the protection of the history of mankind.

The Crystal Skulls

Chapter 17: Nazca Lines

The famed Nazca Lines, located in the desert about 200 miles to the south from Lima, Peru, provide massive geoglyphs depicting creatures such as insects, spiders monkeys, sharks, as well as flowers. The lines are straight and include 800 with 70 plant and animal patterns, and 300 geometric figures. the biggest glyph stretching up to 200m in length, with the longest one being nine miles. The lines are perfectly precisely straight, while others are parallel and interspersed with the appearance of as if they were ancient runways for airports. The plain measures 37 miles in length and one mile wide, with these etched diagrams and lines. They have lasted through the changing climate due to the lack of erosional winds temperature ranges between 80-100°C during daylight hours, and drop to 30° in the evening.

They were discovered around the second half of the 20th century, when planes flew over the desert to bring food and supplies to the desert. Nazca Lines Nazca Lines are between the cities that are located in Nazca and Palpa located in central of Peru. These lines are thought to be the work of the Nazca civilization about 100 BC. They were steadfast and erected an underground system of aqueducts in order to secure an existence that was sustained in a drought-prone, dry climate. The rituals were ceremonial in which they prayed for drinking water as well as their crop to grow. In the blink of an eye, their town was quickly abandoned. There was any physical evidence to indicate why they left their home.

Researchers at researchers from the University of Dresden, in Germany studied the lines, and have determined their magnetic field. They noticed variations on some lines near Nazca and the conductivity measurements were made directly in these lines. The results showed that electrical conductivity was 8000 times greater in the line than adjacent to them. This means that there exist unusual magnetic field variations that are that are located about 8 feet below certain lines. Radiocarbon dating, which was performed on these large drawings shows that they existed in the past, long before Nazca civilization. The researchers are not able to determine their origin or purpose with certainty.

There are many theories about the significance of these devices and their purpose. The experts believe that they may be utilized for reasons of astronomy like following the sun's path, making constellations and even calendar cycles. Some theories also include the use of ancient art or religious motives, as well as the ancient means of communicating across generations. There is a claim that the lines trace the underground water supply sources within the area. There is a belief that they were created to serve as landing areas to

UFOS or other old aircraft in the shape of runway markings. These lines and figures are at a scale of proportion that is only visible at a higher elevation. The discovery has been a source of confusion for all scientists since 1930's because no one has any definitive answers.

Peru Nazca Lines

Monkey (The Nazca Lines)

Chapter 18: The Piri Reis Map

The original document, drawn in 1513 by the Ottoman Turkish admiral Piri Reis geographer and cartographer, was a globe map that was created on the collection of around 20 maps. Through a series of dialogues about the map, Reis compiled and copied data from the source maps, ones that date from about the time of 4th century BC or prior. The map depicts the detailed terrain and maps of the American continent, with precision such that many believe it that it was a result in aerial photography. At that point of time there weren't any aircrafts on the earth and the technology of the time was restricted.

Piri Reis drew sketches of the largely unknown part in South America, notating rivers mountains, lakes and rivers which were unexplored at the time in the past. The map he created depicted North Africa, the coast of Brazil as well as the western shores of Europe. He also illustrated some of the Atlantic Islands such as the Canary Islands, and the Azores, and possibly Japan. The map is only one-third complete. map remains today. However, due to the quality of the drawings depicted, it is an issue of intense debate among scholars.

The discovery of this archeological treasure was made in 1929, as part of the renovation of Topkapi Palace in Istanbul, Turkey. The discovery became an international phenomenon, since it was the first known duplicate of a map of the world from Christopher Columbus, and the one map from the 16th century which showed South America's exact longitude in relation to Africa. In addition, he illustrated the geographical features of Antarctica by mapping it prior to the ice began covering it in the absence of ice. The Antarctica map showed the northern portion of the continent being charted prior to the ice covering as well as the coastline hidden by the frozen sea. This suggests that some one knew, possibly an intelligent civilization what the Earth looked thousands of years ago, from in the sky.

Theoretically, there are numerous theories about various theories about Piri Reis map, with one is on whether or not the map's creators the access to drones or aerial surveys that might have charted Antarctica in the past when there was no ice. There is a belief that a lot of people from ancient times traveled from one pole to the next and could have traveled through Antarctica Antarctic while the oceans were unfrozen, maybe using a navigator which was accurate in determining longitudes. A different theory suggests that the maps used that are used for The Piri Reis map might be attributed to Minoans as well as Phoenicians who were proficient sailors throughout the world of ancient. The source documents and charts might have been transferred to and made available to Constantinople. The city has no definitive explanations for the exactness of this map or what it is that made it possible to create. The location is within the Library of the Topkapi Palace in Istanbul, Turkey.

The Piri Reis Map

The Piri Reis Map Antarctica

Chapter 19: Taos Hum

Taos Hum mystery reports Taos Hum mystery reports began in the late 1950's when the reports included an incessant high-pitched pulsation that was heard throughout the auditorium. The "Hum" occurred in specific regions, including Bristol, England, Taos, Mexico, Bandi, Sydney and Windsor, Ontario. The ELF (extremely Low Frequency) noises were heard by about 2percent of the people living within a zone of hum-prone. The hums were more intense at night but faded throughout the day. Investigations were conducted to determine potential causes, such as the events in these zones However, there was not a reason for this sound that could be explained by science.

Some people experienced nausea, headaches and suicidal tendencies like suicides that occurred in the 1990's, which were attributable to the hum. There were complaints of a constant pounding beat, whining, unsettling sound that drove them to night-time sleeplessness as well as depression. The noise is perceived to the naked ear is called the sound of a diesel engine idle with a variety of sound-detecting systems aren't able to discern it. Scientists confirm that there aren't any underlying natural cause to explain it. They deny it to be an underlying psychotic disorder or perhaps hypochondria.

There are a variety of possible theories for the cause of this audio, such as wireless communication equipment, electromagnetic radiation electric lines, seismic activity or even military research. Most of these claims haven't been linked to mechanical or electrical reasons. In 1993, Congress was asked to study the root of this problem. In 1997, the Congress named scientists and researchers conduct tests on the noise. Initial results showed that the hum is abrupt and starts with a frequency that is always low There are variations within the hum.

There is a possibility that it has connection to the technology used in military communications called ELF. Infrasound may cause effects similar to the noise of hum. It could be an auditory magnetism.

Theoretical theories have been suggested including alien communication or the sound produced by alignments between the planets. There are even spirits who may travel to another side. The Hum can be heard in the indoors but is also heard in rural areas. But the reality of the origins of the audio, The Taos Hum, is a fascinating mystery, whose the origin and reason for existence are not known.

Depiction Of Taos Hum

New Mexico, Taos Hum

Chapter 20: Voynich Manuscript

The Voynich Manuscript was a long-standing document that was written in the 1400s in the beginning, written with a gazelle parchment skin using a language which was not previously been seen or understood. It is filled with vivid images depicting plant-like animals, as well as heavenly drawings. About 240 pages is organized into a sequence of paragraphs which is illustrated and accompanied by diagrams and illustrations. The subject sections comprise scientific, astronomical, biochemical medicinal, herbal, as well as details on pharmaceuticals, as well as 20-30 glyphs, which comprise the bulk part of the texts. The text is free of errors, corrections, or any pauses.

Carbon dating can be a clue to the manuscript being composed between 1404-1438. However, there is no way to determine the identity of the person who wrote the work. The script was acquired through an antiquarian book seller named Wilfrid Voynich, in the year 1912. It has been the subject of numerous unsuccessful attempts at decoding the book. Because the details of the book remain obscure, a variety of theories have been put forward to explain its purpose. Some believe that it is an ancient pharmaceutical publication that depicts therapies for medicine. Some believe it's a sort of cosmological diagram, for instance, a chart of stars or a book written by an alien being. Many believe that it's fraudulent and can't be identified.

The businessman of Finland, Viekko Latvala, who has spoken out and said he's deciphered the book that revealed its secrets. The man describes himself as an "prophet of God". He says the author of the text was an expert in astrology and astronomy. He also studied pharmacy, astronomy and also plants. He studied the plants for the use of their health or scientific properties. Latvala claims that humans are the only ones who will be able to decode the language, it is it a "channel language of prophecy." The author's dialect was a distinct Babylonian dialect. He also claims that the sounds that are in the book comprise a blend of Spanish as well as Italian. He claims that the writer was the one who invented his language. The original text from the Voynich Manuscript can be found at Beinecke's Rare Books as well as the Beinecke Rare Book Manuscript Library. The text is mysterious to this day.

Voynich Manuscript

Chapter 21: "Wow"! Signal

in 1977 Jerry Ehman, a employee of the SETI Project(The Search for Extraterrestrial Intelligence) from Ohio Wesleyan's Perkins Observatory, was scanning radio waves coming from space. His measurements reached their highest at a time that lasted for a period of 72 seconds. The signal appeared to originate in the Sagittarius constellation. It was located close to the star Tau Sagittari located 120 light years from the earth. The signal was detected at precisely the right speed that it couldn't be misinterpreted as noise and wouldn't be interrupted during the journey.

Incredulous, Ehman wrote the word "Wow"! On the printout sheet that attracted media attention and became known by"the "Wow"! Signal. Every attempt to find the signal have been unsuccessful. The source and significance of this signal have caused a lot of debate. Some believe that it could be the first contact with the extraterrestrials of an extremely advanced society. In 2012, around 10.000 Twitter messages were broadcast towards the location the signals originated, however, there was no communication.

The Center for Planetary Science, in 2016, proposed the idea of a comet, or its hydrogen cloud may have created"the "Wow"! signal. The researchers conducted 200 observations within the radio spectrum region from November 2016 and February 2017. The findings of their research confirmed that cometary spectra can be detected at 1420 MHz. They also determined that the "Wow"! signal came from an "natural phenomenon from a solar system body."

The "Wow"! Signal

As a conclusion, the unsolved questions posed by researchers, scientists as well as technological breakthroughs of the present have not been solved yet. The puzzles continue to surround the historical findings, and even with our extensive experience as a civilisation there remain mysteries about which we have no answers. The book aims to provide insight into the subject. If you enjoyed the book, I've created a number of other ebooks about ancient discoveries. They are titled The Ark of the Covenant: New Releasing Discoveries, The Bermuda Triangle Unexplained Absences Beneath the Waves, The Dead Sea Scrolls Ancient Secrets Unveiled Easter Island The Mystical "Stone Giants", The Shroud of Turin The Scientific Evidence, Stonehenge The Mysterious Megaliths And many more. Humanity will always be able to face the issues of the past as well as the in the future by using their imagination and technological capabilities to solve the mysteries of the universe.

www.ingramcontent.com/pod-product-compliance
Lightning Source LLC
Chambersburg PA
CBHW051728020426
42333CB00014B/1213